YOUTH UNEMPLOYMENT AND STATE INTERVENTION

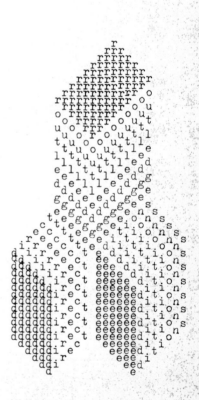

YOUTH UNEMPLOYMENT AND STATE INTERVENTION

Teresa L. Rees and
Paul Atkinson

ROUTLEDGE DIRECT EDITIONS

Routledge & Kegan Paul
London, Boston, Melbourne and Henley

First published in 1982
by Routledge & Kegan Paul Ltd
39 Store Street, London WC1E 7DD,
9 Park Street, Boston, Mass., 02108, USA,
296 Beaconsfield Parade, Middle Park,
Melbourne, 3206, Australia, and
Broadway House, Newtown Road,
Henley-on-Thames, Oxon RG9 1EN
Printed by The Thetford Press,
Thetford, Norfolk

Library of Congress Cataloging in Publication Data

Youth unemployment and state intervention.
(Routledge direct editions)
Bibliography: p.
Includes index.
1. Youth - Employment - Great Britain - Addresses,
essays, lectures. 2. Manpower policy - Great Britain -
Addresses, essays, lectures. I. Rees, Teresa L.
II. Atkinson, Paul.
HD6276.G7Y64 1982   331.3'4137941   82 - 16629

ISBN 0-7100-9263-6

CONTENTS

ACKNOWLEDGMENTS

The idea for this collection of papers arose originally from the shared interest in youth unemployment in the Sociological Research Unit, Department of Sociology, University College, Cardiff and the William Temple Foundation, Manchester. We should like to thank our colleagues in Cardiff and Manchester for their help and support in producing this collection, in particular Gareth Rees and Sara Delamont for their advice and encouragement. Special thanks are due to Myrtle Robins, to whom fell the unenviable task of typing the various chapters.

NOTES ON CONTRIBUTORS

Paul Atkinson is a lecturer in Sociology, University College,
Cardiff. His publications include 'The Clinical Experience'
(Gower, 1981), 'Medical Work: Realities and Routines' (ed.)
with Christian Heath (Gower, 1981), and 'Prospects for the
National Health' (ed.) with Robert Dingwall and Anne Murcott
(Croom Helm, 1979). He is editor of 'Sociology of Health and
Illness'.

Dan Finn was a member of the Centre for Contemporary Cultural
Studies Education Group which produced 'Unpopular Education'
and has written extensively on the history of schooling and
the politics of education. He has recently completed a study
of the transition from school to work in the Salford Inner
City for the Department of Environment with Graham Markall
at the William Temple Foundation, Manchester Business School.
He is currently unemployed.

Denis Gregory is a lecturer at Ruskin College, Oxford. He is at
present seconded to the Wales TUC working on a feasibility
study of Workers Co-operatives. His research work has been
on labour market analyses, work organisation and youth unemployment.

Graham Markall has been carrying out research work at the
William Temple Foundation on youth unemployment in inner
cities and the growth of MSC Special Programmes. He recently
co-authored a report with Dan Finn on Salford for the Department of Environment. He is currently working for the Distribution Industrial Training Board.

Geoff Mungham is a senior lecturer in Sociology at University
College, Cardiff. He is the co-author of 'Images of Law'
(1976), and co-editor of 'Working Class Youth Culture' (1976)
and 'Essays in Law and Society' (1980), all published by
Routledge & Kegan Paul.

Christine Noble was educated in Germany and at Paisley College.
She was a research officer at the William Temple Foundation
on an MSC sponsored project on the trades-unions response to
youth unemployment. She is currently a full-time mother.

Gareth Rees is a lecturer in the Department of Town Planning,
UWIST, Cardiff. His research interests are in the political

economy of urban and regional development. He is co-editor
(with Teresa L. Rees) of 'Poverty and Social Inequality in
Wales' (Croom Helm, 1980) and joint review editor (with
Teresa L. Rees) of 'Sociology'.

Teresa L. Rees is a research fellow in the Sociological Research
Unit, University College, Cardiff. She has conducted a number
of EEC funded studies on aspects of youth unemployment in Wales,
Ireland and N. Ireland. She is co-editor (with Gareth Rees)
of 'Poverty and Social Inequality in Wales' (Croom Helm, 1980).

David Shone graduated in Sociology and Psychology and then completed an MSc on The Social Organization of Seminar Talk at
University College, Cardiff. He was subsequently employed as
a Research Assistant, undertaking an ethnographic study of
industrial training units for young unemployed. He has published papers on the sociology of language and industrial
training.

Howard Williamson graduated from University College, Cardiff in
1975 and subsequently carried out research on young offenders
and the juvenile justice system. He is currently research
officer in the Department of Social and Administrative Studies,
University of Oxford where he is working on an MSC sponsored
project evaluating the Youth Opportunities Programme.

ABBREVIATIONS

BSC	British Steel Corporation
CBI	Confederation of British Industry
CEP	Community Enterprise Project
DES	Department of Education and Science
DHSS	Department of Health and Social Security
DMC	District Manpower Committee (of MSC)
EEC	European Economic Community
ESD	Employment Services Division (of MSC)
JCP	Job Creation Programme
MSC	Manpower Services Commission
NATFE	National Association of Teachers in Further Education
NEDO	National Economic Development Organisation
NFER	National Foundation for Education Research
NUPE	National Union of Public Employees
OPDP	Oldfield Painting and Decorating Project
PBWE	Project Based Work Experience
SLS	Social and Life Skills
SPD	Special Programmes Division (of MSC)
STEP	Special Temporary Employment Programme
TGWU	Transport and General Workers Union
TOPS	Training Opportunities Scheme
TSA	Training Services Agency (of MSC - now TSD)
TSD	Training Services Division (of MSC)
TUC	Trades Union Congress
USDAW	Union of Shop Distributive and Allied Workers
UVP	Unified Vocational Preparation
WEEP	Work Experience on Employers' Premises
WEP	Work Experience Programme
YMCA	Young Men's Christian Association
YOP	Youth Opportunities Programme

Chapter 1

YOUTH UNEMPLOYMENT AND STATE INTERVENTION

Paul Atkinson and Teresa L. Rees

INTRODUCTION

No observer of contemporary Britain can fail to be aware of the
emergence (or re-emergence) in recent years of mass unemployment.
Levels of employment and unemployment are constantly brought to
popular attention: the weekly loss of jobs is featured on tele-
vision newscasts and in the local and national press; worsening
levels of unemployment receive detailed coverage; concern is
fuelled with the publication of each month's official figures;
increasingly gloomy projections for the future are published. Unemployment, 'the recession' and economic crisis are now deeply em-
bedded in popular consciousness. They define the horizons for
political debate.
    Within the context of worsening employment, the particular
plight of young people has been identified as a subject for special
concern. School-leavers' job prospects have worsened dramatically
in recent years. Just as in the 1930s (see chapter 2) anxieties
are expressed as a twin concern for a waste of the nation's resources and the demoralisation of youth, potentially leading to a
variety of antisocial behaviour. This concern is translated into
positive discrimination in favour of young people in the state
response to unemployment. The Manpower Services Commission (MSC),
set up in 1974 to foster training and employment services, has
grown enormously as a state agency, particularly in the area of
providing special temporary measures to combat unemployment - and
most of these have been directed towards young people. The impact
of the MSC has indeed mushroomed to such an extent that it is anticipated that one in two of all the 1981 cohort of school-leavers
will spend some time on its main special endeavour, the Youth
Opportunities Programme (YOP).
    Despite the impressive scale of MSC's activities, in terms of
quantity of opportunities offered of work experience and training,
it remains a relatively small organisation. Unlike most other
spheres of government activity, the MSC depends upon the co-operation of other state sectors (particularly education) and semi-state
bodies as well as the trade-union movement, local government, the
private and voluntary sectors. The MSC acts, then, as a mobilising

1

agent: it shapes the problem and the solution. While remaining a modest-sized organization, in terms of staff and overheads, it distributes the resources whereby a massive programme of schemes are actually implemented by other organisations. And it should be remembered that the resources of the MSC actually come, in the main, from the EEC Social Fund - a euphemism for a training programme.

The way in which the state has responded to the problem of youth unemployment, both in Britain and in other free market economies, represents a unique form of intervention in the workings of the labour market. The extent to which the MSC has managed to mobilise goodwill and co-operation is quite remarkable. On the other hand, it can be argued that in providing temporary opportunities in a worsening economic climate the MSC is simply starting with the wrong premise, and as such its activities, however well intentioned, are no more than a cosmetic irrelevance.

This volume identifies a number of key issues in the pattern of state response to youth unemployment which has evolved in the inter-war (see chapter 2) and post-war period, concentrating in particular on the decade when the problem, and the response have intensified. We examine the question why young people in particular have been singled out for special governmental attention. Unemployment has grown for all groups and has been particularly severe in some regions and some industries among adults with the financial commitments of family responsibilities - what is so politically significant about school-leavers? (See chapters 2 and 3.) Why has the MSC channelled resources into providing work experience for young people at the expense of its other functions of training and placing? (See chapters 3 and 9.) What is the nature of the relationship of the special programmes with the education sector which is both expected to make an input to YOP (paid for by the MSC) and yet is experiencing substantial cuts in its own budget? (See chapters 4 and 9.) What is the response of the trade-union movement to the programmes, how can it both co-operate with the government in combatting youth unemployment and yet ensure that members are not 'displaced' by school-leavers on work experience? (See chapter 6.) And what are the reactions of the young people themselves on special programmes? (See chapters 7, 8 and 9.) In addressing ourselves to these questions we chart the changing nature of the state responses to youth unemployment since 1974 as it becomes increasingly recognised that the 'problem', far from being a temporary one, is potentially permanent (see chapter 5). In this chapter we set the scene by describing briefly the young people's labour market in this period and by examining the role of special measures in the government's package of policies to combat unemployment. We compare the general approach with those taken by other European countries facing similar problems. And finally we identify the 'moral panic' over youth unemployment as a major impetus for the unprecedented level of involvement in the labour market in recent years by both labour and conservative administrations.

YOUNG PEOPLE'S LABOUR MARKET IN THE 1970s AND EARLY 1980s

Young people are always particularly vulnerable to unemployment in
a recession, largely due to cuts in recruitment (and to a lesser
extent 'last in, first out' redundancy practices); the 1974 recession was no exception and it was in this year that levels of youth
unemployment began to rise dramatically. The problem was exacerbated by a growth in labour supply in the 1970s due to a variety
of factors: the growth in the number of school-leavers joining
the labour market (as a result of the 1960s' 'baby boom'), the
increased economic activity rates of married women (from 42 per
cent in 1971 to 57 per cent in 1979) and the fact that fewer than
average people reached retirement age (due to a trough of births
in the 1914-18 period).
    Changes in the industrial structure of employment over the last
decade have exacerbated the problem, rendering young people's employment prospects particularly bleak. Those sectors which young
people traditionally enter when starting work for the first time,
such as manufacturing, distribution, transport and communication -
together accounting for 60% of first time entrants (MSC 1977a) -
are exactly those industries which have experienced the greatest
number of net job losses in the past decade. Makeham's study of
youth unemployment using national statistics ascribes much of the
growth in the 1970s to cuts in recruitment and demonstrates a 1
per cent rise in overall male unemployment to be associated with a
1.7 per cent rise in young men's unemployment. Girls' prospects
are even more sensitive to the general problem as a 1 per cent rise
in overall female unemployment was found to be associated with a 3
per cent rise in young women's unemployment (Makeham, 1980).
    Levels of youth unemployment have risen throughout Britain but,
like adult unemployment, it is not distributed evenly. Regions
with a rundown economy such as the North, Scotland, Wales and the
North East have the highest figures. Similarly, particular categories of young people, irrespective of their geographical location, experience disproportionately high levels of unemployment.
Ethnic minority groups, for example, have more difficulty in obtaining employment even when the economy is buoyant, and this is compounded when jobs are scarce as in the period 1973 to 1977 when
the number of unemployed 16- and 17-year-olds from a commonwealth
background trebled. The handicapped also suffer disproportionately
whatever the state of the economy and whether the nature of the dis-
ability be mental, physical or both. Finally, girls have more difficulty than boys partly because women have tended to be ghettoised
in certain industries that are declining rapidly (such as textiles)
and when competing with boys in traditionally male employment, they
are likely to experience discrimination. Female youth unemployment
grew far more rapidly than that of males in the 1970s and whereas
males under 25 constitute 30 per cent of all registered male unemployment, the corresponding figure for young women is 52 per cent.
    While ethnic minorities, the handicapped and girls may be ex-
periencing particular difficulty in getting a job, the situation
has become increasingly problematic for all groups, in all areas.
The extent of the problem is underestimated in the official figures
because some young people, particularly among West Indians, do not

register. However, from the figures that are available, the growing
severity of the problem is illustrated by the extent to which the
periods of unemployment experienced by young people have been
lengthening. Characteristically, school-leavers have spent their
early years in the labour market chopping and changing jobs and
sometimes these changes have been interspersed with brief periods
out of work. These periods have lengthened in recent years so that
young people now comprise a major proportion of the long-term
unemployed, a group traditionally made up of much older workers.
Long-term unemployment has increased proportionately far more among
young workers than among other age groups, and for many of these
people the experience of unemployment preceded the experience of
employment.

In the early days of MSC's operations, it perceived its role as
helping young people to overcome the disadvantage they suffered in
competing for jobs with older workers - lack of experience. It was
felt that school-leavers were discriminated against by employers
in a period of labour surplus because they could offer no experience or references, and, given minimum wage agreements, were not
significantly cheaper. The MSC identified this 'vicious circle'
as the chief cause of youth unemployment. In order to avoid disillusion and alienation setting in among young people, the MSC
sought to break the 'vicious circle' by offering a temporary period
of sponsored work experience, originally on the Work Experience
Programme (1976 to 1978) and subsequently on YOP (which also provides training opportunities).

Had the original premise that youth unemployment was a temporary
problem held true, then this strategy might have proved effective.
It could have sharpened school-leavers' competitive edge even if it
did not actually increase the number of permanent jobs. However,
as the economic decline has deepened and structural unemployment
become entrenched, so there are more and more opportunities for
temporary work experience and training, but fewer and fewer jobs
for which young people may compete. Increasingly school-leavers
are 'progressing' from one temporary opportunity to another until
they are too old to benefit from YOP. The increase in the MSC's
budget and concomitant growth in the number of opportunities has
kept the levels of youth unemployment stable in the last three
years in that YOP trainees are temporarily removed from the unemployment register. However, the fundamental problem, that of a mismatch between a permanent, structural problem being treated by a
temporary, piecemeal solution, remains.

In many European countries the same picture emerges. Debates
about coping with youth unemployment are couched in terms of numbers of places on special schemes, the quality of training and
education inputs, the matching up of opportunities to unemployment
blackspots and positive discrimination in favour of the disadvantaged young job seekers. However, as we suggest in the next section, special temporary measures are an inappropriate strategy for
the state to adopt for a problem whose permanence is politically
unacceptable.

TEMPORARY PROBLEM, TEMPORARY SOLUTION

It is clear that in the mid-1970s the 'problem' of escalating youth
unemployment which faced most EEC member states was perceived as
a temporary one linked to demographic changes and a short-term
recession. Forms of state intervention in response to the problem
came under two broad headings: reduction of labour supply and job
creation measures, both direct, as in temporary schemes (such as
the Work Experience Programme) and indirect, through the injection
of capital. In the UK the emphasis was on temporary direct job
creation measures. Elsewhere such measures were introduced in addition to limiting the labour supply (e.g. Belgium, France) and
capital investment programmes (such as that of the Republic of
Ireland in the public sector).
     Methods of limiting the labour supply have involved both the re-
moval of certain categories of people from the labour force and reducing the hours, weeks and years worked by members of it. In
common with other member states, Britain did, of course, raise the
school-leaving age (in 1974) which served to stave off the problem
of a cohort of school-leavers entering the labour market for at
least a year. Other member states also have compulsory national
military service of, on average, a year's duration and overseas
voluntary programmes providing for rather more than the 1,500 to
2,000 young people from the UK who are so involved each year. The
'guest worker' system which operates in many EEC countries theoretically enables the state to 'export' part of its unemployment
problems: a controversial scheme for the voluntary repatriation
of immigrant workers has been proposed in France.
     More significant, however, are the measures that other member
states have introduced to reduce the time spent by people in the
labour force, and it is here that Britain's response to unemployment differs. Early retirement is the measure which the largest
number of member states have tackled. In Britain the Job Release
Scheme was introduced whereby workers who retire early are entitled
to an allowance, provided the employers concerned take on a young
unemployed person as a replacement. It was extended in 1981 from
64 for a man and 59 for a woman to the ages of 62 for a man and 57
for a woman. However, its impact in 'freeing up' jobs is still
clearly marginal.   By contrast, a similar scheme operating in
Belgium created 22,657 jobs between January 1976 and January
1979 by reducing the ages from 65 and 60 to 60 and 55.   Other
attempts in Britain to reduce the retirement age have been unsuccessful.
     All EEC member states have been gradually reducing the standard
number of hours worked per week so that 40 now appears the EEC norm.
The UK stands out as having the longest working week (46.5 hours).
Some member states have reduced the weekly working hours to 38 or
36 in some industries and are extending annual leave to 6 weeks.
     Job creation schemes of one sort or another have been introduced
in all EEC member states as well as Canada, the US, Australia and
elsewhere. The schemes come under three broad headings: subsidies
to private sector employers; training programmes; and temporary
direct job creation measures.
     Three types of subsidy to private sector employers can be identi-
fied: subsidies leading to the creation of new jobs (e.g. Belgium,

France, Ireland and Denmark);   subsidies offered to employers for
recruiting preferentially in favour of disadvantaged job seekers
(West Germany, Netherlands, France) and subsidies to defer redundancies and support short-time working (France, Germany, Italy and
Luxembourg). Britain has long been propping up the textile industry through the Temporary Employment Subsidy and other industries
through the Short Time Working Subsidy. A subsidy for employers to
take on young people was introduced in 1975 (the Recruitment Subsidy for School Leavers) only to be replaced in 1976 by another
scheme (the Youth Employment Subsidy) which was scrapped in 1978.
A new scheme is due to be reintroduced in 1982 (the Young Workers
Scheme) whereby employers are given a contribution towards the
cost of employing an under 18-year-old for the first year provided
the unfortunate person is not paid in excess of £45 per week.
   Some countries, for example, Austria, Switzerland and West
Germany, have used an expansion of the apprenticeship system as a
means of reducing school-leaver unemployment. In each of these
three countries, the proportion of school leavers entering apprenticeships exceeds 50 per cent. Unlike the UK, apprenticeships are
not confined to traditional male/craft industries, and programmes
include general education and training. In the UK there has been
a decline in the number of apprenticeships offered, allied to the
demise of those manufacturing industries where apprenticeships are
concentrated. In response the MSC introduced an apprenticeship
award scheme in 1975; when this subsidy ceased a further decline
in numbers followed. A further 1,500 grants were awarded by the
MSC to support first-year apprenticeships in 1980-1 and the intention is to maintain this level of provision.
   In the UK the primary response to rising levels of youth unemployment has been a series of special measures introduced by the
MSC to create temporary jobs and provide a period of work experience. They are perceived as a temporary solution to a temporary
problem and share the following common features with similar
schemes abroad:
   1 projects must be 'additional', i.e. they must not be tasks
      public bodies are statutorily obliged to carry out anyway,
      or, in the case of the private sector, must comprise the
      undertaking of work which would not otherwise be done;
   2 the projects must be non-profit making;
   3 in some cases a further education or training element is
      provided;
   4 in some cases positive discrimination is exercised in re-
      cruitment in favour of the young, the long term unemployed
      or regional blackspots.
The MSC special measures began with the Job Creation Programme
(JCP) in 1975 and the Work Experience Programme (WEP) in 1976: they
were originally given a life of three years. Meanwhile the Holland
Committee was set up and produced its report in 1977 (MSC, 1977a)
which recommended the setting up of the Youth Opportunities Programme (YOP) which would provide a range of training and work experience opportunities for the under 19-year-olds. At the same
time, a direct job creation scheme, the Special Temporary Employment Programme (STEP) would provide work for the 19- to 24-year-
olds. YOP and STEP were set up in 1978 and have seen a range of

changes in rules and additions in budget. STEP finally closed down in 1981 to be replaced by the almost indistinguishable Community Enterprise Programme (CEP) aimed at the long-term unemployed.

The main aim of YOP is still to help young unemployed people to gain permanent employment as soon as possible. All unemployed school-leavers are guaranteed the offer of a suitable opportunity on the programme by the Easter following their leaving school. In addition anyone under 19 who has been unemployed for 12 months is to be offered a place within 3 months. The participants on the programme are regarded as MSC's trainees and as such receive an allowance, currently £23.50 per week, which is exempt from tax and national insurance contributions. Trainees are entitled to day release for further education. Places on YOP normally last for 6 months and school-leavers are entitled to a period of up to 12 months on YOP provided they have been unemployed continuously for six weeks or more.

YOP is made up of two broad types of 'opportunity': work experience and training. The majority of placements offer the former and most of these are on Work Experience on Employers' Premises (WEEP) whereby young people spend six months with an employer learning a range of tasks. In 1980-1 two-thirds of the sponsors of WEEP were private sector employers in establishments with less than 10 employees, mostly in the service sector or, to a lesser extent, manufacturing. Local authorities and other public bodies provided a further 30 per cent of places and the remainder came from voluntary and charitable organisations. The role of the private sector in sponsoring WEEP places has diminished compared with previous years.

Project Based Work Experience (PBWE) and Community Service (CS) schemes tend to offer about 12 and 40 places respectively on specific projects 'of value to the community'. PBWE projects tend to involve physical work such as environmental improvement or creating a play area, while CS tends to involve placing trainees in existing organisations such as old people's homes.

The other arm of YOP's activities is broadly described as work preparation. It is made up of training workshops, most of which are sponsored by local authorities, and a number of courses such as Short Training Courses, Employment Induction Courses and Work Introduction Courses, all designed to improve the employability of different categories of young people.

In 1978-9 the work experience schemes provided 64 per cent of placements on YOP, but by 1980-1 this has grown to 84 per cent, and most of these are on WEEP. The impact of YOP on youth unemployment has grown significantly. In 1978-9 it provided a stop gap for 1 in 8 school-leavers but by 1981-2 the programme is coping with half of all school-leavers: it has become an institutionalised feature of young people's post-school experience of the labour market. The proportion of trainees leaving YOP who are placed in permanent employment has dropped to around 30 per cent. While YOP plays an increasingly important role, it is still only a temporary programme.

State response to youth unemployment is characterised, then, as a series of extensions and modifications to a set of temporary measures. In chapter 5 Markall and Gregory outline two strands which can be identified in the MSC's response: the accommodative and the

transformative. They elaborate on the extent to which state intervention has been informed by fears for social and political disruption as unemployment levels rose. They illustrate how MSC has
been sufficiently flexible to be able to adapt to the entrenchment
of high levels of unemployment but only through these programme
modifications, not by tackling the underlying problem. It is
noticeable that as unemployment passed one major benchmark at 2
million and is now approaching 3 million, the MSC, while subject to
budget restraints in the general round of public expenditure cuts,
has actually been given expanded resources and been encouraged to
develop new schemes and initiatives.

In 'caring' for and about the marginalised 'failures' among unemployed youth, the MSC's 'special measures' effectively translate
the political and structural problems into technical or organisational issues, in the provision of 'places', the distribution of
resources and so on. The activities of the MSC have helped to
create a climate in which the economic and social problems of youth
unemployment have been transformed into a comparatively consensual
approach. 'Solutions' can be pursued through the co-operation of
employers, unions, statutory and voluntary agencies. It is, to a
large extent, an exercise in the mobilisation of goodwill. (This
is not to say that this has been an entirely trouble-free process.
Goodwill has worn thin in several quarters - not least from the
trades unions: this is outlined in chapter 6.)

However, as Markall and Gregory go on to suggest, the MSC has
developed more than just this palliative function. It has taken on
a more directive role - and a more obviously political one - in what
they refer to as its 'transformative' mode. Rather than confining
themselves to crisis management, the MSC has taken on the task of
restructuring the work-force. It has been arrogating to itself the
job of changing the skills, values and experiences of an increasingly large proportion of school-leavers in Britain. Some particular
aspects of this transformative intervention are examined elsewhere
in this collection - including attempts to remedy the supposed 'deficiencies' of unemployed youth.

THE 'MORAL PANIC' OF YOUTH UNEMPLOYMENT

Part of the recurring rhetoric in discussions of youth unemployment
has been couched in terms suggestive of 'moral panic'. That is, as
Mungham puts it in chapter 3, 'unemployed youth have always been a
special cause for concern over and above the obvious fact of their
being without work.' Rees and Rees show (in chapter 2) that in the
1930s youth unemployment was seen, as it is now, as a waste of the
nation's resources and as leading to the demoralisation of the young
people. However, one wonders whether there would have been either
then or now quite the same frenzied debate or level of intervention
had it not been for the fear that this demoralisation would lead to
crime, riots and other forms of damage to the social fabric. Such
youth has been portrayed as a fertile seed-bed for racial unrest,
and as the target for political agitation, from extremists of both
right and left. They are, in one telling phrase quoted by Mungham,
seen as 'the nation's rotting seed corn'.

Rees and Rees demonstrate that just as mass unemployment is not a new phenomenon in Britain, so too the response, in terms of rhetoric and action, has been remarkably consistent. Hence the contemporary social problem is not a one-off crisis, born of a short-term recession but has indeéd been a recurring crisis. Rees and Rees outline from an historical perspective the changing nature of 'state intervention' in this field. One of the most remarkable features is the extent to which contemporary approaches to youth unemployment mirror and recapitulate earlier formulations. One can read pre-war documents which are all but indistinguishable from recent statements emanating from the MSC. The chapter by Rees and Rees provides an historical background to the subject matter of this volume.

The perspective of youth unemployment as a moral panic has been given particular force by actual manifestations of social unrest in Britain in 1981, in the riots in Liverpool, Manchester and London. The contributions to this book were substantially complete before those riots took place, and before the subsequent commentary, inquiries and recriminations. But the response to such social disorder has been in accordance with the perspectives outlined by Mungham.

In most quarters the riots of 1981 have indeed been interpreted in line with two major 'panics' - race relations and youth unemployment. These have been coupled with expressed anxiety over the state of policing - especially in the 'inner city' areas - and hence with ever present fears over the maintenance of 'law and order'.

Here we are not concerned primarily with establishing whether the riots were 'really' the product of widespread youth unemployment: by the same token we make no attempt to deny any relationship between the two. Rather, we wish to point out how popular and political response to such disorder expresses and amplifies anxieties which have attended 'the problem' for years. They have been given extra force and urgency by the advent of riots, but are by no means novel. As Mungham points out, the social control of youth is a focus for a broader set of fears concerning social order, whether the immediate 'trigger' be mugging, football hooliganism, political extremism, drug abuse or whatever.

It may be thought that the most recent riots undermine Mungham's argument, that 'the problem of youth unemployment is ... a thing of no substance.' But as he himself goes on to remark, this is not to deny the possibility - or the reality - of sporadic outbursts of violent behaviour. The suggestion is rather that this is likely to be incoherent, aimless violence, rather than the sort of co-ordinated political activity which is predicted by the moral panics. The 'pointless destruction' is unlikely to crystallise into sustained social action.

Increasingly, of course, the fears concerning social disruption have been seen to be justified by outbreaks of rioting. They have appeared to confirm the warnings and prognostications referred to by Mungham. They have given a new urgency to the provision of state intervention programmes - especially in the 'depressed' areas. They have also sharpened the image of 'demoralised' workless youth.

The 'demoralisation' of the unemployed - the young in particular - is again a common and recurrent preoccupation. This topic is ad-

dressed by the authors of chapter 9. They concentrate on just one
element of contemporary intervention - the so-called 'social and
life skills' element of the Youth Opportunities Programme. As the
name implies, training of this sort is designed to equip otherwise
unemployed youngsters with sets of skills and knowledge in order to
'cope' with everyday life, and with working life in particular. As
the authors of the chapter suggest, the rhetoric informing this variety of intervention embodies a 'deficit' model of the workless adolescent. They point to parallels with 'compensatory' education.
The young person is portrayed as lacking in certain sorts of capacities, which is seen as either cause or consequence of 'failure'
to find work. In chapter 9 Atkinson et al. are critical of this
element of YOP, claiming that it embodies an inappropriate, and misleading ideology. That is, it deflects attention away from the
structural aspects of the problem, and displays the all too common
tendency to 'blame the victim'. The unemployed youngsters are made
the scapegoats for their own 'failure' to enter long-term employment. This chapter therefore highlights the dominant theme of this
book: how the construction of the 'problem' foreshadows and deter-
mines the form of 'solutions'.

It is worth reiterating here that one immediate response to the
1981 riots was the announcement of a massive increase in state resources made available for the Youth Opportunities Programme.
Directly or indirectly such state intervention is regarded as one
available mechanism of social control. As is pointed out in chapter 9, its air of 'moral rearmament' is central to such a control
strategy.

The young people themselves are not the only scapegoats. The
education system has also been incriminated as contributing to 'the
problem'. Young people are described as being inadequately or inappropriately prepared for the adult world of work. This has resulted in two main consequences. First, the MSC interventions have
rapidly begun to comprise an 'alternative' form of training and
educational experience. While in most contexts recent years have
witnessed cuts and contractions in educational provision, the MSC
has, in effect, been able to bypass the Department of Education and
Science and expand post-compulsory educational opportunities of
certain sorts. Indeed, such has been the expansion (following increasing numbers of jobless school-leavers) that we have now seen
a de facto raising of the school-leaving age (in itself a tried
cosmetic procedure) to relieve pressure on the labour market.

The second consequence for education has been a concerted attempt
to tighten the bond between education and the world of work. The
relationships between education and employment in general has been
a topic for debate between sociologists and economists of education,
and it is taken up in some detail in the contribution from Dan Finn
(chapter 4). He rehearses debates concerning education's proper
contribution to the 'needs' of industry, and to the 'employability'
of school-leavers. In many ways, the demand for more 'relevant'
schooling is less a matter of technical skills and qualifications,
more a 'moral' question. The appropriate socialisation which is
demanded is primarily a question of the inculcation of 'the right'
attitudes and values. The implications of state intervention are
not only attempts to alter the distribution and availability of work

and training, it also implies the transformation of identities within the work-force.

It is, therefore, highly pertinent to pay some attention to interventionist programmes' impact on young people themselves. Such a consideration provides the theme for the two chapters by Markall and Williamson (chapters 7 and 8). They provide us with much needed insight into what schemes can be like in practice, and some understanding of the 'consumers'' viewpoints. Their chapters rely on in-depth case studies of specific projects. Given the number and diversity of such projects throughout the country in recent years, it is impossible to claim that these case studies can be treated as 'typical' or 'representative' of them all. No such claims are made here. On the other hand, it is possible, through such investigations, to raise and illuminate issues which are generic, even though their local manifestations vary.

CONCLUSION

We have argued that the fundamental flaw in the state response to youth unemployment is its perception of the problem as a temporary one. While discussions of the success of YOP in terms of numbers of places provided have recently given way to discussions about the quality of experience and training provided, it is clear to young people among others that while YOP may be a temporary alternative, it is no solution to unemployment.

The MSC has recently launched a consultative document entitled 'A New Training Initiative' (MSC, 1981d) one of whose objectives was that all young people under 18 should have the opportunity either of continuing in full-time education, or of entering training, or a period of planned work experience combined with related training and education. The response from industry inter alia has been largely to pose the question 'who will pay'? MSC now seem unclear whether to go for more state intervention by providing a better training scheme for young people that will eventually replace YOP, or to revert to insisting that the burden of responsibility for training should lie with employers - a decision to retain some of the Industrial Training Boards illustrating some support for this view.

Sir Richard O'Brien (the MSC chairman) in a recent speech demonstrates this quandary by stating that 'reliance on the free market would lead to a deficiency in the quality and quantity of training' and yet an increase in direct government intervention as a provider is 'not necessarily the answer'. The issues now to be resolved according to O'Brien are as follows:

whether the state should assume responsibility for financing, through general taxation, the transition from school to work via some learning period which would attract an allowance on the lines of the Youth Opportunities Programme;

whether employers individually or collectively, via a levy system, should pay for skills training without direct state support;

whether the state or the employer, or both, should fund adult training and retraining.

O'Brien also asks whether training should be provided by a statutory system such as the Industrial Training Boards, or reliance
be placed on voluntary arrangements.

It is clear, then, that an administration which believes in a
free market economy has nevertheless felt it necessary to ensure
that unemployed school-leavers are prepared for a world of work.
Resources for YOP have been increased substantially in recent
years and now a major revamp of the programme is on the cards.
The image of alienated, anti-social young people is still sufficiently powerful to jolt the government into some sort of action,
while maintaining the view that the problem is but a temporary
one.   There is little indication among either of the main political parties, or the trades unions, or any of the organisations,
public and private, that the MSC relies upon, of a shift from the
view that there is a world of work for which to prepare young
people.

Chapter 2

JUVENILE UNEMPLOYMENT AND THE STATE BETWEEN THE WARS

Gareth Rees and Teresa L. Rees

As Britain's economic crisis has deepened through the 1970s and into the 1980s, so the state's commitment to the maintenance of 'full employment' — conceived in the optimism of war-time reconstruction planning — has become a mockery. Generations of workers who grew up during the long boom after 1945 have been introduced to the awful reality of mass unemployment; whilst for many of those entering the labour market for the first time now, to be jobless is a perfectly routine feature of their world. It is unsurprising, then, that the experience of the years between the wars — the last period of comparable economic desolation — has become an increasingly commonplace point of reference, not merely of the politician's rhetoric, but also of more sober academic analyses (for example, Seabrook, 1981; Pimlott, 1981).

These latter have frequently argued the doubtful value of such parallels: and certainly the 1980s are not the 1930s. The extent and structure of unemployment are very different now. The past fifty years have seen the wholesale restructuring of the British economy and a dramatic deterioration of its international competitiveness. Moreover, there have been fundamental changes in the character of the British state — and in the social relationships which underpin it — not least, of course, in response to the inter-war crisis itself (Jessop, 1980).

However, this does not argue that nothing can be learned about the contemporary situation from an examination of the earlier period. Indeed, it is the purpose of this chapter to draw precisely such lessons from an analysis of a particular issue — juvenile unemployment — which, then as now, was an important focus of political and popular concern. Hence, irrespective of the changes which have taken place, there are straightforward similarities in the responses of the state to the problem of unemployment amongst young people during the two periods. More importantly, however, there are major analytical continuities. Simply put, we believe that the development of state responses to juvenile unemployment between the wars should be understood in the much wider context of the relationships between class groupings which characterised British society during a period of rapid and far reaching economic reorganisation. The form of those responses embodied the

definitions of the issue constructed by those interests which were
dominant;   their implementation was an admittedly small part in
the resolution of the conflicts between these class groupings,
largely on the terms of the dominant interests. We think that it
is exactly this kind of analysis which also provides the key to un-
lock the seeming mysteries of policy on youth unemployment during
the contemporary period and which are discussed elsewhere in this
volume.

THE SCOPE OF JUVENILE UNEMPLOYMENT BETWEEN THE WARS

From the scanty information available, it would appear that juvenile unemployment did not reach serious proportions in the years
preceding the First World War (Garside, 1977). In so far as public
concern was expressed over young people's work, it focused on the
quality rather than the quantity of jobs available. Edwardian
commentators were especially vexed by the prevalence of 'blind
alley' occupations, such as the 'errand boy' (for example, Tawney,
1909). The fear was that many school-leavers were being attracted
by relatively high wages into employment requiring little or no
skill, only to be dismissed as they reached their eighteenth birth-
days and entitlement to adult wages and replaced by new school-
leavers. Hence, it was argued that many young workers achieved
adulthood with no marketable skills and their prospects of future
employment perhaps permanently impaired.

   This controversy clearly echoed earlier concern over the 'boy
labour' problem, which had been stressed, for example, in the 1886
'Report of the Royal Commission on the Depression of Trade'. And
it continued to be an issue during the inter-war years (for example,
Gollan, 1936). It was felt that the rapid expansion of the distributive trades (and services more generally) had enlarged a key
source of such occupations. Similarly, a number of contemporary
studies criticised the exploitation of cheap juvenile labour in
traditional industries such as cotton (Jewkes and Winterbottom,
1933;   Jewkes and Jewkes, 1938) and coal mining (Gollan, 1936).
Even the new, consumer-orientated industries, which were growing
in the South East and Midlands of England were not immune, although
here it was as much the general 'deskilling' which flowed from the
introduction of Fordist techniques of production which was of concern. For example, the 'Report of Juvenile Employment' of 1934
commented: 'the new factory work is purely repetitive, and offers
no real prospects of advancement, even if it offers continuity of
employment beyond 16 or 18 years of age' (Ministry of Labour, 1934a,
p.4). Nevertheless, the priority of concern shifted after the First
World War to include the mounting problem of juvenile unemployment.

   Initially, this problem was conceived as the temporary consequence of the transition from the war-time economy to the conditions of peace. Munitions production had created large-scale
employment for young people, in which high wages could be earned,
albeit in recompense for working very long hours at boring, repetitive tasks. Clearly, as the Lewis Committee pointed out, many of
these young boys and girls would be out of a job when the munitions
industry was run down in the post-war years (Lewis Committee, 1917).

And as it transpired, these fears were more than amply borne out.
For instance, one estimate claimed that over half of the juveniles
thrown out of work at the armistice were unable to obtain alternative jobs (Seymour, 1928).

The available data make it difficult, however, to establish the
overall consequences of the re-establishment of a peace time economy (Garside, 1976). It would appear that by 1923 some 79,000
young people (under 18 years of age) were registered with Divi-
sional Employment Exchanges and Juvenile Employment Bureaux in the
United Kingdom; and this figure had only fallen to a little over
64,000 by 1927 (Garside, 1977, Appendix III). Nevertheless, there
was a significant improvement in the general trend of unemployment
for boys and girls during the second half of the decade, although
this masked wide variations between particular localities and
regions - a point we shall return to later (Garside, 1977, Appendix I). Moreover, it was confidently expected that the situation
would continue to improve as a simple consequence of demographic
changes. Hence, the Local Juvenile Employment Committees of the
Ministry of Labour argued that the depressed birth rates of the
First World War would be reflected in the decline of juveniles presenting themselves for work between 1928 and 1933, although again
there might be local variations (Ministry of Labour, 1929;
quoted in Garside, 1977, p. 329). All in all, it was thought,
there would be a natural evaporation of juvenile labour surpluses.

Of course, what had not been adequately foreseen was the extent
to which general levels of industrial activity would be depressed
after 1929. The result of the economic crisis of the early 1930s
was that total unemployment rates in Britain - as elsewhere - rose
dramatically; not surprisingly, juvenile unemployment reflected
this trend. Hence, unemployment amongst insured boys (clearly an
underestimate of the total out of work) rose from just over 3 per
cent in 1929 to over 8 per cent by 1932; for insured girls, it
more than doubled from 3.1 per cent to 6.3 per cent during the same
years. In fact, it was only with the general improvement of trade
after 1933 that these rates began to fall significantly; although,
it should be remembered that as late as 1938 over 4 per cent of
insured 16- and 17-year-old boys and some 5 per cent of such girls
remained out of work (Garside, 1977, Appendix I).

Accordingly, it was during the early 1930s that the most acute
problems of juvenile unemployment were posed, at least in so far as
these were reflected in the aggregate, British statistics. However, as we have already suggested, this general picture obscures
very major local and regional contrasts. The essential point here
is that the structure of unemployment during the years between the
wars was highly regionalised. Apart from the recession years of
1921-2 and 1929-33, severe unemployment was confined to those areas
of the north and west which were dependent upon the crisis-ridden
staple industries (textiles, coal, iron and steel, ship building,
etc.). And regional contrasts became especially pronounced with the
growth of consumer-based industries in the South East and Midlands
of England (for example, Pollard, 1962).

Quite simply, the incidence of unemployment amongst young people
mirrored this pattern (Garside, 1977, Appendix II). In this way,
the experience of boys and girls in the labour market diverged

sharply, depending upon where they happened to be brought up. For
example, South Wales was wholly dominated by coal mining, with particular localities given over to iron, steel and tinplate production. Given the recurring difficulties experienced by these industries - and coal in particular - throughout the inter-war years, it
is not surprising that the region suffered levels of unemployment
amongst boys which were amongst the highest in Britain (Garside,
1977, Appendix II). Moreover, so precarious was 'King Coal' at
this time that contemporary studies record a growing unwillingness
amongst youngsters to work underground. As the 'Second Industrial
Survey' (National Industrial Development Council of Wales and Monmouthshire, 1937) commented:

> their parents' past experience of unemployment and short time
> is the main reason why boys are reluctant to enter the indus-
> try.... Boys are said to ask for any employment 'except under-
> ground', and while at one time they preferred mining employment
> to transfer outside South Wales, there are now many instances
> of a reversal of this point of view (vol. 3, p.11).

For girls the situation was rather worse: the region simply
offered few employment opportunities outside of the distributive
trades and domestic service. And, as we shall see later, this
latter was very often a route out of the region altogether. Hence,
the exceptionally high rates of unemployment amongst Welsh girls (in
spite of non-registration of many more) were a clear expression of
these restricted opportunities (Garside, 1977, Appendix I).

Moreover, there were even more local variations in the incidence
of juvenile unemployment. For instance, in December 1933, admittedly when total levels of juvenile unemployment had fallen, no less
that 20 per cent of young people recorded as out of work were to be
found in Liverpool, Glasgow, Bristol, Manchester and Newcastle
(Ministry of Labour, 1933). Thus, the character of juvenile unemployment between the wars reflected not only the cyclical variations
in the British economy as a whole, but also the complexity of local
and regional employment structures. Both these, in turn, were important conditions, shaping the nature of state responses to the
problem.

THE CONSTRUCTION OF STATE POLICY ON JUVENILE UNEMPLOYMENT

The statistical account given in the previous section provides a basic
background against which to analyse state responses to juvenile unemployment between the wars. However, in itself it cannot explain why
successive administrations felt compelled to develop policies to treat
the issue; neither can it account for the form of those policies. To
begin to address these questions, we need to examine the way in which
juvenile unemployment was perceived by contemporaries: that is, to examine the social construction of the phenomenon as a societal problem,
meriting specific policy initiatives. What, in short, was the ideology of juvenile unemployment which actually underpinned state policies?

It would appear that there was a considerable degree of consensus
amongst what may be termed the 'policy-framing elites' of the inter-
war years as to the nature and consequences of juvenile unemployment.[2] At one level, it was a straightforward economic problem:
it implies a waste of the nation's resources, as well as a weaken-

ing of the future labour force through a failure of so many young
people to acquire the necessary vocational skills. Hence, for example:

> It is hardly too much to say that, by exposing this generation
> of industrial workers to the most deadly effects of the present
> depression we are storing up elements which threaten to perpet-
> uate depression by striking at the quality of future labour re-
> sources (Jewkes and Winterbottom, 1933, p. 15).

However, much more significant were the moral dimensions of the
problem. Consider, for example, the following passage from a contemporary account of juvenile unemployment in South Wales:

> Two arguments emerge which cannot, it is claimed, be contra-
> dicted: (a) that juvenile unemployment is a more serious matter
> than adult unemployment and (b) that so far as juvenile employ-
> ment is concerned, much of it must be regarded with disquiet in
> so far as it is non progressive and offers no training to the
> juveniles engaged therein that fits them for future employment.
> Both these features of juvenile life attack morale, inculcate
> bad habits, breed dissatisfaction, and hinder the full blossom-
> ing of personality. Ultimately they produce a generation of
> people not amenable to discipline and unable to stand on their
> own feet; filled with desires which crave satisfaction, but
> not knowing how or where realisation might be sought; demand-
> ing a remedy, but totally uncritical of the nostrums offered by
> competing physicians; men and women, in a word, called to citi-
> zenship but without understanding the responsibilities implicit
> in the response to that call (Meara, 1936, p. 109).

What is clear here is that prolonged periods of enforced idleness
were seen as undermining the employability of young people, not
only through a literal deterioration in their physical capacities,
but more fundamentally by preventing the inculcation of the stability and disciplines of the work ethic and by stifling the growth
of appropriate aspirations and self esteem.

In many ways, then, this concern with the 'demoralisation' (as
it was routinely described by contemporaries) of the young unemployed echoed that earlier, Victorian preoccupation with the 'demoralisation' of the urban working class (especially in London:
Stedman Jones, 1971). And, again in parallel fashion, 'demoralisation' amongst young people was associated during the inter-war
years with wider social disintegrations. In individuals it was
linked in many minds (although not universally: Morgan, 1939, pp.
170-1) with increased delinquency. Thus the Chief Constable of
Newport:

> unemployment, giving rise to the lack of pocket money, often
> persuades young people into the path of crime. In order to
> obtain amusement and diversion from their idleness, these of-
> fenders turn to pilfering for funds to buy cigarettes, attend
> the cinema, etc. Once the first step is taken in this direc-
> tion, an early escape from detection soon encourages a repeti-
> tion of this easy means of acquiring the desired money or petty
> luxuries (County Borough of Newport, 1933, p. 3).

Collectively, 'demoralisation', it was feared, would manifest in
political extremism and social disorder. As Meara (1936) again
puts it: 'Enforced idleness leads ultimately to demoralisation, to

loss of pride in one's own person and appearance, to envy of those
better placed in society, and envy leads in the last resort to
social conflict' (p.19). And, of course, there had been quite extensive youth riots, directed largely at the police, in various
parts of London during July and August 1919, which may have provided a tangible impulse to these fears.[3]

This definition of the problem of juvenile unemployment implied
two objectives for state policies: to manage what were believed to
be the deleterious and even dangerous consequences of unemployment
amongst young people; and to reduce the actual incidence of such
unemployment. Given the more or less persistent view that juvenile unemployment was a temporary phenomenon, it was the former
objective which was accorded most weight in public pronouncement:
and, certainly, it is this objective which most closely corres-
ponds to what has been regarded as the major element of the state's
response - the Juvenile Unemployment Centres/Junior Instruction
Centres.[4]

Juvenile Unemployment Centres were first established during 1918
as a temporary expedient to cope with the problems of the transition to peacetime conditions. However, the scheme was resusci-
tated in 1920 and put on a more permanent basis, when it became
possible to make attendance at a centre a condition of receipt of
unemployment benefit. Persistent attempts at reform during the
1920s culminated in a 1930 reorganisation, when the centres became known as Junior Instruction Centres. Nevertheless, it was
nqt until the Unemployment Act of 1934, when age of entry into
unemployment insurance was lowered from 16 to 14, that local education authorities were compelled to make some sort of educational
provision for the young unemployed and the young people themselves
were obliged to attend the centre or class provided.[5]

The ethos of the centres may be gauged from the following passage
from a circular letter from the Ministry of Labour in 1930: the aim
of the policy was:

> by inculcating habits of discipline and self respect and giving
> some instruction both of a practical and academic character, to
> increase their adaptability and to make them more capable of
> accepting any suitable employment which may be offered them.
> At the same time, while this may be ideal, it is held that
> attendance at a class which provides any form of organised in-
> struction is better than loafing about the streets (Public
> Records Office Lab. 19/60; quoted in Pope, no date, p.10).

Similarly, a memorandum from the Minister of Labour four years
later described the purposes of the scheme as:

> the prevention of demoralisation ... to give the boys and girls
> a real interest in life, to keep their minds and fingers active
> and alert and their bodies fit, to teach them something which
> will be of real use to them whether at home or work, and, with-
> out trying to train them for specific occupations, to give them
> the type of mental and manual instruction which will help them
> to become absorbed or reabsorbed into employment as soon as an
> opportunity may occur (Minister of Labour, 1934, p.4).

In short, the aims of the centres were nothing more than the pre-
vention of 'demoralisation' and the maintenance of 'employability'
through an emphasis upon the work ethic.

To this end, the centres provided a curriculum which was predominantly practical, without being vocational: for the boys, wood-
work, metalwork, boot repairing and leatherwork; for the girls,
cookery, dress-making and home nursing. In later years, this
pretty basic diet was supplemented with physical training and games;
as well as, in some centres, drawing and painting, drama, civics,
English, arithmetic and history (Morgan, 1939).[6]

Given this orientation, it is perhaps unsurprising that the 'dole
schools', as they were known, acquired an enduring unpopularity
amongst those required to attend them, as is suggested by the high
levels of absenteeism. As one contemporary commentator put it:

> I have asked many whether they would rather be at work than at
> school, and hardly ever was there one who professed a preference
> for school. They are the unlucky ones who are robbed of their
> liberty, they think. Their friends have the job which is the
> stamp of manhood and womanhood; they have their few shillings
> to spend on the pictures or going to a dance; they can have
> their flutter on the pools or save up for a new blouse or a
> fresh tie. But these unfortunates, bereft of all these desir-
> able things, are kept in the old-time bondage of the school
> house with its association of subordination to other wills and
> set ways (Morgan, 1939, p.97).

This association with school must have been reinforced by the
fact that many centres were housed in abandoned elementary schools;
although these were amongst the better facilities, at least until
the 1934 reorganisation occasioned the widespread adoption of new
premises. Moreover, the centres were equally unpopular with staff,
who resented the low status accorded to this work within the educational world, as well as the ever present threat of losing their
job if numbers attending fell below the necessary minimum.

The Juvenile Unemployment Centres/ Junior Instruction Centres
were, then, essentially preventative, negative institutions, reflecting with extreme clarity an ideology of juvenile unemployment
which was preoccupied with the threat which it posed to the smooth
operation of economy and society. This quality was clearly perceived by many of those who attended the centres: Jeremy Seabrook's
Blackburn respondent who, many years later, suggested that the 'dole
schools' existed 'to keep us off the streets' (1973, p.202) had it
about right. Moreover, the centres were limited simply as a consequence of the limited numbers of young people who passed through
them.

Two points should be made here. First, there was by no means a
centre in every locality where there were significant levels of
juvenile unemployment. Hence, a peak was reached in 1931 when
there were a mere 180 centres in the whole of Britain; by 1937,
three years after the legislation making some kind of provision
compulsory, there were only 175 centres and classes in England and
Wales and a further 53 centres and classes in Scotland. The central
problem here was one of finance; many local authorities, burdened
by unemployment and declining rate income, were unhappy with a
Ministry of Labour grant of only 75 per cent of the costs of a centre
(with the exception of the mining districts, where 100 per cent
grants were paid; a provision extended to other very depressed
areas after 1934).

The second point is that, even where centres were available, only a small proportion of unemployed young people ever attended. For example, in the peak year of 1931, the highest attendance figure was 21,162; the average figure of recorded unemployment was some 115,000. By 1937, the equivalent data were 27,449 and 86,100 (Morgan, 1939; Garside, 1977, Appendix III). Most obviously, at least until 1934, attendance by uninsured 14- and 15-year-olds was extremely patchy, simply because it was voluntary. But even after 1934, a large proportion of those appearing on the unemployment register were not eligible to attend a centre, whether because they had left school too recently, had been unemployed for too short a period or for some other reason. It is striking that a Ministry of Labour survey in February 1936 revealed that even had all the centres necessary been in existence, no more than half the unemployed juveniles on the live register could have been required to attend (Ministry of Labour, 1936).

In short, then, it was clearly never intended that the scheme should have a major impact upon the mass of unemployed young people; it was designed to reach only a small fraction of them. It is much more difficult, of course, to say what the impact of the centres was upon those who did experience them: however, there is certainly no evidence to suggest that they found getting a job any easier, a factor which probably contributed to the centres' unpopularity. All this makes it rather surprising that there was not greater debate and controversy over the 'dole schools' and their functioning. Certainly, what debate there was more often than not treated the Juvenile Unemployment Centres/Junior Instruction Centres as one aspect of a much more inclusive policy programme, the key element of which was perceived to be the school-leaving age.

The 1918 Education Act had established the minimum school-leaving age at 14, whilst granting local education authorities the right to make by-law extension up to 15. In fact, this latter power was not used, in spite of the fact that large numbers of young people did stay on at school voluntarily, in preference to unemployment (for example, Meara, 1936). Accordingly, the basic issue became whether there should be a national extension of the leaving age to 15.·

During the earlier years of the 1920s, the principal advocates of extension were those who saw it as simply one element in the general struggle to improve the access of working-class children to the 'upper' (i.e., above elementary) levels of the educational system (Centre for Contemporary Cultural Studies Education Group, 1981). And the rationale which stressed the removal of unwanted youngsters from the labour market was a secondary one. Indeed, successive administrations proved unwilling to extend compulsory education in large part because it was viewed as a far reaching educational issue. For example, a report of the Juvenile Organisation Committee of the Board of Education concluded in 1924:

> It would appear ... a point for consideration whether questions
> of important and permanent educational developments can fairly
> be dealt with primarily from the point of view of measures de-
> signed to meet a special industrial problem. There may even be
> some danger lest, by hasty improvisation to bring such develop-
> ments into operation at an early date as a remedy for unemploy-

ment difficulties, permanent educational advance may be pre-
judiced (Board of Education, 1924, quoted in Garside, 1977,
p.326).

Thus, both conservative and labour led governments could reserve
the evanescent problem (as it was persistently viewed) of juvenile
unemployment for remedy by means of the Juvenile Unemployment
Centres.

However, in the latter part of the decade, events conspired to
change these policy alignments quite considerably. In the face of
mounting unemployment, the labour movement as a whole (including
the parliamentary party: Barker, 1972) became committed to raising
the school-leaving age as a weapon against juvenile unemployment:
indeed, it was claimed that the consequent withdrawal of 400,000 to
500,000 young people from the labour market would reduce unemployment amongst 16- and 17-year-olds to negligible proportions, create
vacancies equivalent to 85,000 adult jobs and save the unemployment
fund between £9 million and £12 million (Tawney, 1928). This
transformation, however, should be interpreted in the context of
developments in the more general world of educational reform. Most
significantly, the Hadow Report of 1927 recommended a school-leaving age of 15, as part of a much wider reorganisation of elementary
schools. It thus became much easier to emphasise the employment
arguments for a policy which was already officially acceptable in
educational terms. Moreover, the civil servants of the Board of
Education became more sympathetic to calls for extending the school-
leaving age in the context of the Hadow Report, which had proved
acceptable to the labour movement despite its stopping a long way
short of the complete abolition of the elementary secondary school
division (for advocacy of this latter view, see Tawney, 1922).

Most interestingly of all, sections of the employers also came
to see the value of extending the school-leaving age as a means of
combating unemployment. In particular, those 'advanced' sections
of industrial capital associated respectively with the liberal
party and, for example, the Conference on Industrial Reorganisation and Industrial Relations became associated with advocacy of
the reform. And finally, during the 1930s, the 'corporatist' elements within the conservative party itself – personified in Harold
Macmillan – adopted the extension of schooling as part of the educational reform which was seen as an integral element of their programme of national reconstruction. Nevertheless, it was not until
1936 that action was actually taken, with the announcement that
the school-leaving age would be raised within three years; and,
even then, given the predominant ideology of the government, this
reflected political expediency rather than a commitment to social
reform (Simon, 1974).

The significance of this – to all intents and purposes – abortive
attempt to alleviate the juvenile unemployment problem lies in the
light which it casts upon the process of state policy making. What
it highlights – in a way in which the Juvenile Unemployment Centres/
Junior Instruction Centres do not – are the relationships between
the groupings within the 'policy framing elite' which provide the
essential context of policy development. In the most general terms,
it has been suggested that:

> The 1920s and 1930s saw a particularly bitter struggle between
> two contending alliances. The first, oppositional alliance
> was organised around the demand for egalitarian forms of edu-
> cational expansion; the second, dominant alliance resisted
> these demands and sought, where possible, to reverse expan-
> sionist tendencies (Centre for Contemporary Cultural Studies
> Education Group, 1981, p.41).

And, as we have seen, the issue of raising the school-leaving age
came to be closely bound up with this conflict over the reform of
the whole school system.

However, alignments were clearly much more complex than the
quotation suggests, as its authors themselves recognise. Hence,
for example, within the 'oppositional alliance', centred on the
organisations of the labour movement, the reforming programme was
compatible with either a thorough-going educational egalitarian-
ism or a more elitist, meritocratic concern with 'equality of opportunity' and, in reality, both orientations were represented within
the alliance (Barker, 1972). Moreover, ambiguities of this kind
were reflected in the acceptance by the labour movement of the
partial reforms recommended by the Hadow Committee, as well as in
the advocacy of the extension of compulsory schooling in terms of
its unemployment rather than educational benefits. Equally, although the core of the 'dominant alliance' was provided by the
employers' organisations and the conservative party, we have shown
that sections within these groupings became committed to educational reform, whether generally or as a specific response to juvenile unemployment. And in effect, it was this coaslescence of
disparate forces in support of the raising of the school-leaving
age that created the essential conditions for the announcement of
1936 and, more importantly, the major educational reforms of the
1940s.

What is equally significant is that the dominant terrain of the
debate over the school-leaving age was set in terms of the requirements of capital. Hence, the educational arguments for an extended
period of schooling were, to a large extent, displaced by those
relating to unemployment. Keeping children out of the labour market
when they were an inconvenience could be justified as easily as
ensuring an adequate supply of labour had been a few years earlier
when there were local shortages of young workers because the prime
consideration was not what would benefit the young people, but what
would benefit the economy. And, significantly, this was true just
as much of the organisations of the labour movement, as it was of
those of capital. Moreover, exactly parallel arguments can be made
in respect of the third element of state policy on juvenile unemployment, the Industrial Transference Scheme.

The Industrial Transference Scheme was aimed at facilitating
the movement of workers from areas of labour surplus to areas of
labour shortage; during the inter-war period, this meant migration
from the depressed areas of the north and west to the growth regions
of the South East and Midlands of England. It was a policy which
precisely reflected the contemporary economic theory with regard to
what was an appropriate response to unemployment: move somewhere
else (Pitfield, 1973; 1978).

The scheme was begun in 1927 as a means of transferring miners
between coalfields and into industries other than mining.   In the
following year, the Industrial Transference Board was set up with
more extensive powers to ease inter-regional movement: job vacancies were notified between regions;   training for new jobs was
provided;   and subsidies were made towards the costs of moving.
The scheme remained confined to the depressed mining regions, although some areas where the major industries were iron and steel or
ship building were included;   after 1934, the whole of the newly
created special areas became eligible (Pitfield, 1973).   Very substantial numbers of workers were moved through the scheme, although
by no means as many as moved voluntarily.   Indeed, Pitfield (1978)
has argued convincingly that Industrial Transference was widely
viewed as the most efficacious element of the state's response to
the regional unemployment problem, at least until the late 1930s.
The transference of young people was a major part of the scheme.
As can be seen from table 2.1, large numbers of boys and girls were
moved under the Juvenile Transference Scheme, introduced in 1928
for the former and 1929 for the latter.   In addition, many young
people must have moved as part of the Household Transference Scheme,
which provided subsidies for the removal of the families of adult,
male transferees;   whilst Family Transference, introduced in 1935,
facilitated the movement of entire families, where younger members
had obtained work in new areas (Owen, 1937).

TABLE 2.1   Labour transference 1928-38

	Total individuals	Boys	Girls	Households and family removals
1928	n.a.	1,840	n.a.	–
1929	43,698	2,622	1,994	2,850
1930	33,031	1,313	1,708	2,100
1931	23,374	868	1,986	1,680
1932	14,140	628	2,502	990
1933	13,443	1,117	2,955	605
1934	16,421	1,661	3,512	1,308
1935	29,753	5,375	4,648	3,718
1936	43,506	9,449	5,958	10,025
1937	38,125	7,675	6,450	7,673
1938	27,627	4,131	5,496	4,000

Source: adapted from Pitfield, 1978, table 3, p.431

It was, of course, the Juvenile Transference Scheme which shared
most with the other aspects of state policy on juvenile unemployment.
Hence, for example, it was associated with an extensive programme
of 'training' schemes which bear comparison with the Juvenile Unem-

ployment Centres/Junior Instruction Centres; although again by no
means all transferees attended. At the most basic level was a
Ministry of Labour system of Junior Transfer Centres: residential
camps which were intended to restore the physical capacity of young
people to undertake hard work. Somewhat similar 'reconditioning
camps' were organised for the Ministry by the Young Men's Christian
Association (YMCA) which, with a regime of physical training, games
and swimming, and elementary handwork, were aimed at 'building up
a boy's body (and) help(ing) to pull him together after a long
spell of unemployment' (Morgan, 1939, p.87).[7]

More significant, perhaps, were the quite extensive arrangements
made for the vocational training of potential transferees. Hence,
for example, the YMCA ran a number of training centres which had
originally been developed to equip boys for farming in the Domin-
ions. Similarly, the YMCA and the Boy Scouts Association trained
boys for service in hotels and clubs and for the catering trade
(Morgan, 1939).

For girls, there was a much more extensive system, organised
after 1920 by the Central Committee on Women's Training and Employment, directed almost exclusively at training for domestic service
(for which there was always a ready demand). In addition to five
residential centres, there was a network of day centres concentrated
for the most part into the areas of worst unemployment. For example,
in South Wales there were day centres at Aberdare, Abertillery,
Bargoed, Cardiff, Garnant, Maesteg, Merthyr Tydfil, Mountain Ash,
Neath, Pontypool, Pontypridd, Swansea and Tonypandy (Board of
Trade, 1932).

The essential consequence of the Juvenile Transference Scheme
was the movement of many thousands of young people out of the depressed areas to those where there was a demand for labour. The
latter comprised not only those areas where new manufacturing
industries were developing, but also those prosperous residential
and recreational centres (such as seaside resorts), especially in
the south of England, where there were openings for domestic servants.[8] And, it should be remembered, the Transference Scheme
merely contributed to an already existing and much larger flow of
young people to those places where the prospect of employment was
better.

For many transferees, of course, migration was swiftly followed
by a return home: one Ministry of Labour investigation set the
'coefficient of wastage' for the scheme as high as 35 per cent.
For only a proportion of these, their return represented a rejection of the scheme, whether for reasons of 'culture shock', dislike of their new job or whatever (see Daniel, 1940, Appendix I for
some graphic accounts of the difficulties experienced by some Welsh
transferees to Oxford). For others, family circumstances, the
availability of work in their home locality and so forth provide
the explanation for their return. More generally, even amongst
those transferees who stayed the course, there remained a considerable hostility aroused by the circumstances which forced them
to enter the scheme and the conditions which they thereby had to
endure. This is expressed with great clarity in the quotation
which follows, in which a former domestic servant reflects upon
her own experiences:

It was the poverty that gave them servants. No pride in appearance, no new clothes. It was us in Wales and in different parts
like Northumberland. Our mothers were glad (they weren't glad
to see us go) for us to go to a meal of food and for someone to
clothe us, 'cause they couldn't.... It was heartbreaking ... and
they - what was the word now? They exploited us, more or less
(Mrs Jennie Owen's oral testimony, quoted in Taylor, 1979,
p.139).

For the communities which yielded up the young transferees, the
loss of large numbers of young and frequently talented people was,
of course, a critical blow to their futures and aroused the bitterest resentment. Even the largely unsympathetic Sir Wyndham Portal
was moved to comment in his report to the Ministry of Labour on
the industrial conditions of South Wales and Monmouthshire:

At many meetings which I attended I found a measure of resentment
that the young and able bodied should be in necessity of leaving
the district to find employment ... the view was held that the
government should, as an alternative to transference, take essential steps to obtain control and direction in the allocation of
new industries, having regard to the claims of the depressed
areas (Ministry of Labour, 1934b, paras 137-49).

More specifically, many trade unionists objected to the scheme because they regarded it as a means of providing cheap labour for the
expanding industries. This objection applied, of course, to Industrial Transference as a whole: as Professor Marquand put it:

the chief objection raised against transfer has been inspired,
not by nationalist sentiment or even love of home, but by the
reluctance of unemployed men to seek work on conditions which
they feel to be undermining the standards established by workers
in other parts of the country (Marquand, 1936, p.189).

Nevertheless, resentment against newcomers from the depressed areas
was a potent source of social conflict in the expanding areas, where
competition over jobs and wages was compounded by problems of over-
crowding in local housing. Indeed, in Slough and other parts of
London hostilities reached such a pitch that there were actually
street brawls between rival groups of workers. In particular, it
was held that the younger elements amongst the migrants - many of
whom would have moved through the Transference Scheme - were especially ill disciplined and created difficulties even for the local
trades-union organisers; and this was a claim which was often made
against Welsh migrants, who tended to be younger than those from
other parts of Britain. For example, one contemporary commentator
remarked that:

It will require great diplomatic powers on the part of trade
union leaders to overcome the hatred displayed by both north-
erners and southerners towards the Welsh because of their alleged
tendency both to undercut wages and to 'rat' on their fellow
workers (Daly, 1938, p.261).

What is striking, however, is that this widespread hostility to-
ward the Industrial Transference Scheme, and in particular its
effects upon young people, does not appear to have been translated
into opposition to the scheme at the level of the 'policy framing
elite'. This is not surprising, of course, in the case of the
dominant elements amongst the employers' organisations and conserva-

tive politicians (although some disquiet was expressed by, for
example, coal owners over the loss of potential manpower). However, even organised labour - as expressed through the General
Council of the Trades Union Congress and the leadership of the
labour party - appeared to accept that Industrial Transference was
an inevitable response to the economic problems of the inter-war
years. As Hilary Marquand, Professor of Industrial Relations at
University College, Cardiff and to become a labour MP and member of
the 1945 government, put it:

> If there are young men and women who see a reasonable oppor-
> tunity of exchanging the misery of chronic unemployment in South
> Wales for a steady job and an adequate wage in London or Birming-
> ham, then it would be foolish to attempt to prevent them from
> taking that job, merely in order to satisfy the nationalist
> passions of persons who hold safe jobs themselves (1936, p.189).

In effect, Industrial Transference remained the dominant policy
with respect to regional unemployment right up until the mid-1930s.
It was only in the face of mounting unemployment that opposition
grew and, crucially, the alternative policy of moving work to the
depressed regions began to be advocated widely. These pressures to
shift the emphasis of policy began in the labour opposition and
trade-union movement (as expressed, for example, in the debates on
the First Reports of the Commissioners for the Special Areas in
1935). However, the crucial influence probably came from inside
the conservative party itself and from the 'advanced' sections of
industrial capital which saw the need for 'modernising' Britain's
industrial structure and which had been active on the various regional Industrial Development Councils (as, of course, had trades
unionists). Nevertheless, the conservatives who dominated the
government - and in particular Chamberlain at the Treasury - remained unconvinced of the efficacy of the new policies, irrespective of the passage of the 1934 Special Areas Act. Only after 1937
is there any real evidence of a shift in legislative intention and,
even then, the emphasis appears to have been on creating new industries (i.e. restructuring the economy), rather than solving the
problems of regional unemployment (Page, 1977; Pitfield, 1978).

This last point is significant because it is necessary to locate
the whole development of transference policy in the context of the
(albeit fitful) growth of a 'corporatist' state system which itself
was in large measure a response to the central problem of restructuring British industry in the face of the dramatically changed
conditions of the international economy (Middlemas, 1979). To
simplify, in the aftermath of the General Strike of 1926, there
emerged a consensual relationship between major sections of the
employers' organisations and the Trades Union Congress: a consensus which, intermittently and unevenly, had a major effect upon
the formulation of state policy. The Industrial Transference Scheme
was an example of policy which reflected this consensual relationship precisely, facilitating as it did the necessary relocation of
the labour force, which was itself an important condition of industrial restructuring in general (Owen, 1937). Moreover, the
corollary of the 'incorporation' of the central organisations of
the labour movement was the exclusion of the 'grass roots' and
'left wing' elements from decision making within those organisa-

tions (Middlemas, 1979). And it was here, as we have seen, that
the bitterest opposition to transference was voiced.

CONCLUDING COMMENTS

Let us conclude this necessarily preliminary discussion of juvenile unemployment and the state between the wars by summarising
our arguments. We have sought to establish that there were three
areas of state policy which bore upon the problem: the Juvenile
Unemployment Centres/Junior Instruction Centres; the school-
leaving age; and Industrial Transference. If we consider these
areas as one programme, then we have tried to establish the following general proposition. The programme was based upon a particular definition of the nature of juvenile unemployment, which emphasised 'employability' and 'demoralisation'. The programme was
the product of the relationships between class groupings, mediated
through the policy making mechanisms of the state. These relationships should be understood in the context of the emerging 'corporatist' response to the necessity to restructure the British economy.
    We leave it to readers of other chapters in this volume to judge
the extent to which current policies on youth unemployment are
equally class-based responses to the conditions generated in economic crisis.

NOTES

1 We are grateful to Steve Davies and Dan Finn for helpful discussions in the preparation of this chapter.
2 We have in mind here the leaderships of the major political
   parties, employers' organisations and trades unions, the civil
   servants and professionals, voluntary organisations and so
   forth.
3 White (1981) records that 'there was conflict in Greenwich,
   Hammersmith, Tottenham, Edmonton, Wood Green, Barking and
   Brixton and probably elsewhere' (p.260). He suggests that the
   riots were a reaction to the employment situation, with the
   labour market being swamped by returning servicemen; to inflation; and to the police, faced with the task of maintaining
   law and order during a period of relaxation of wartime disciplines and controls.
4 Much of what follows draws its factual basis from materials
   supplied to us by Rex Pope. We are extremely grateful to him
   for his help.
5 The 1930 Scheme provided for the setting up of classes where
   the numbers of juveniles unemployed did not warrant the creation
   of a specialist centre.
6 Some young people, deemed to have special abilities, were allowed
   to attend classes at continuation schools, technical schools
   or schools of art or commerce. The numbers involved were
   very small.
7 In some ways these camps resembled the highly unpopular government instruction camps, which were reserved for the long term

unemployed over eighteen years of age (see, for example, Lush, 1941, pp. 69-71). They were residential camps, run on strict army discipline, frequently in rural areas where the typical work comprised land drainage, afforestation, roadmaking, etc. A contemporary correspondence in 'The Times' compared them with the compulsory labour camps of Nazi Germany (Branson and Heine-mann, 1971, p.43).

8 Domestic service also provided the greatest outlet for trans-ferees within their region; for example, in South Wales there was a not inconsiderable movement from the coalfield to the large urban settlements of the coast.

Chapter 3

WORKLESS YOUTH AS A 'MORAL PANIC'

Geoff Mungham

INTRODUCTION

Unemployed youth have always been a special cause for concern
over and above the obvious fact of their being without work. Historically, workless youth have served as a focus for successive
panics and fears as to the supposed social and political implications of large scale and long term youth unemployment. Young
people in this predicament have been viewed, at different times,
as the 'nation's rotting seed corn', as prime fodder for agitators
coming at them from both Right and Left, and as a potential source
of chronic instability and unrest. Such fears are echoed no less
virulently today. The object of this chapter is to explore the
basis of some of these obsessions about the young unemployed and
to look at the range of warnings, predictions and solutions these
fears have given rise to.
    While no contemporary British politician can avoid making ex-
pressions of regret about the general numbers of unemployed,
nevertheless it is invariably the young workless who bear the
brunt of a special kind of worry and frenzied concern. From
this vantage point it is 'displaced' youth who are seen as being
potentially the most troublesome social segment, as the carriers
of disorder and possible subversion. The following remarks capture perfectly one popular set of phobias centring on the problem
of unemployed youth:
    Young men unemployed today seem very likely criminals and
    political bomb-throwers tomorrow. Crime rates are highest
    for people in their late teens and early twenties, and high-
    est of all for those unemployed minorities among the young
    (blacks, immigrants). Most governments have short, uncom-
    fortable memories of the student ructions of the late 1960s
    and fear that the recruiting sergeants of extremism and revo-
    lution cannot be far away from the jobless young ('The
    Economist', 1977, p.87).
    This sort of social morbidity is of interest on several counts.
In the first place, though the message about the incipient unruli-
ness of youth is one so often repeated that it has come close to
attaining the standard of a universal truth, how real in fact is

the prospect of 'youthful rebellion'?   Second, does the persistent
use of the terms 'youth' or 'young people' as undifferentiated
social categories, dull our appreciation of the intricacies of
the social stratification of the young, and of the implications
of such rankings and distinctions for understanding the complex
social character of contemporary youth?   Finally – and perhaps
most important – do episodic panics about 'youth' carry a much
deeper message about the condition of society and the future of
the social order, as has been suggested elsewhere (Mungham and
Pearson, 1976)?   In this way 'youth' comes to serve as a metaphor
of social change, a vehicle for the articulation of a broader set
of fears about the quality of 'society' and troubling issues. From
this standpoint, if young people are not amenable to reason and
control, then what hope for maintaining intact the entire social
fabric?   It is the persistent recurrence of these themes which
gives the study of youth cultures its special social significance
and a particular point to any examination of societal reactions
to the problem of workless youth.

HISTORICAL CONFIGURATIONS; UNEMPLOYED YOUTH AS PARASITE AND PREDATOR

It is not difficult to trace the preoccupation in Britain since
the industrial revolution with the unemployed or otherwise idle
young.   The vision of workless youth was never primarily one
which saw too many hands that should be put to some productive
use, but rather one where youth unemployment was woven together
with crime, insubordination and moral degeneration into an imagined
dark and threatening alliance.   Some titles from nineteenth- and
early twentieth-century writings on the moral and physical anatomy
of youth convey the prevailing fears well enough.   Neale's (1840)
study of juvenile delinquency in Manchester sought to link crime
with unemployment.   In 1853 the influential 'Prospective Review'
ran a series of articles on the theme of 'Society in Danger From
Children' and in so doing touched on the nerve of supposed gene-
rational tensions.   As Gillis (1974) has pointed out, fears about
the possibility of growing conflicts between the old and the young
were common ingredients in much of the nineteenth-century literature on the 'youth question'.   A study by Phillips (1855) played,
as many others did, on old worries of the 'mob' and the 'dangerous classes', where the unemployed young (Phillips's 'wild tribes')
were alleged to be in the vanguard of subversion.   Similar sentiments were echoed by Osborn (1860), by Pare (1862) and in Letchworth's (1877) report on 'deprived and delinquent children'.   The
same obsessions carried over into the twentieth century, with the
publication of studies such as those by Urwick (1904), Russell
(1905) and Devon (1912) on the notion of 'society' under siege
from groups of unemployed young.   In each case the spectre said
to be haunting the old order were groups of idle, sturdy and
'untamed' (Archer, 1865, p.125) young men – those without work and
who were also held to be without affection for existing institutions and authority.

Archer's worries about the untamed and unruly young were widely
shared. His vision of 'knots of hulking youths' (1865, p.125)
whose spirit was not yet crushed by pauperisation or agencies of
social control, and who were held to be a danger to the social
order, was one endorsed by all those who saw young, single, unemployed men as the greatest threat to civil society. This was the
essence of the fear of the rootless, 'unintegrated', workless rural
and urban proletariat. Chesney's (1970) study of the Victorian
underworld makes mention of the special fear felt for 'regular
munchers' (p.64), a class of 'casuals' - a large group of un- or
under-employed young men who were viewed as the main potential
source for insurrection and trouble. Again, Hobsbawm and Rude
(1969) noted how in the 'Captain Swing' rebellion of 1830, it
was young, unmarried men who were among the most active and militant machine breakers and rick burners, being those who 'received
least from the parish and were most likely to be forced into the
most degrading and useless kinds of parish labour, e.g. on the
road gangs, which provided only too justified centres of disaffection' (p.211).

This fear of resistance from unbridled and 'irresponsible' young
spirits was always a double-edged coinage. On the one hand, if
only the means could be found to harness this energy into respectable channels then youth could not only be saved from itself, it
might also become the source of societal renewal and regeneration
(cf. Urwick, 1904; Gillis, 1974). But on the other hand, the
dominant sentiment was one without hope. Workless youth were here
regarded as the source of contamination of manners, deviance and
corruption, just as surely as bacteria, if untreated, would inexor-
ably infest and destroy otherwise healthy organisms (and we have
to remember that biological analogies of this sort were much in
favour at a time when there was a market for the wilder ideas of
eugenicists, social darwinists and other crude forms of biological
reductionism).

Notions of 'contamination' in this particular context have been
explored by Pearson (1975) who has described a Victorian demonology
about the young which was something akin to a domino theory of
moral sensibilities. Pearson illustrated the Victorians' near
obsessional interest in 'the relationship between crime and poverty,
deviance and class membership, and the relationship of the "dangerous classes" to the labouring population as a whole' (p.154). Once
more we find at the heart of these worries an ancient fear about
the imagined destructive energies of those Thompson depicted as
'loose single men' (1968, p.895) - a fear above all of young men,
with no commitment to or stake in the prevailing order. Pearson
cites Chadwick's concern about the genesis and character of the
urban mobs; according to Chadwick, the truculent rabble busy in
such places as Bethnal Green, Bristol, Liverpool and Manchester,
were made up overwhelmingly of young persons, 'the great havoc ...
was committed by mere boys' (Chadwick quoted in Pearson, 1975,
p.202). For those moralisers and reformers like Chadwick, youth
was dangerous because it was going unsupervised and unregulated,
in large measure because poor health standards and resulting pre-
mature deaths ('of the heads of families') helped produce a British
demography where, for most of the nineteenth century, almost 50 per

cent of the population were under 20 years of age (cf. Tobias,
1967, p.198), and a corresponding 'lapse of staid influence
amidst a young population' (Chadwick in Pearson, 1975, p.201).

The great fear buried in the middle of this declamatory rhetoric was that of the contamination of respectable and industrious
youth (and others), by workless and therefore suspect and subversive youth. Thus by this reckoning, the young unemployed were not
simply a danger to themselves - bad enough though this was - but
also threatened because of their supposed capacity to touch and
corrupt other more orderly and conforming youthful minds. The
idea of a contagion fitted in well with the thinking of those in
nineteenth-century Britain who were ever fearful of keeping un-
tainted the loyalty and fidelity of the labouring classes in
general.

The central strategem for the better control of young single men
which Chadwick and others preached was, of course, sanitary reform.
By this reasoning, if the race could be rendered fitter and sounder,
then the (longer) survival of the eldest would be a valuable corrective ('socialising agents') for the wayward and unattached
young. Sanitary reform could guarantee the family, and the family,
in turn, could monitor its young. But other measures for incorporation were also discussed and implemented. These included demands
for more compulsory schooling on the grounds - not unfamiliar to
contemporary ears - that young people who were neither at school
nor in gainful employment were a risk to themselves and a trouble
for society. The supposed virtues of extra schooling are well captured in the following argument of the day and made in the period
leading up to the first great educational reform act of 1870:

  And what are these neglected children doing if they are not
  at school? They are idling in the streets and wynds; troubling about in the gutters; selling matches; running errands;
  working in tobacco shops, cared for by no one (McCosh, 1867).

As we know, compulsory school attendance - then as now - generated tensions between the authorities and the poor, as the struggle
to civilise and instruct youth sharpened in the nineteenth century.
Other attempts at salvaging youth came via agencies such as the
Oxford Men's and Lads' Institutes set up in the 1880s, various
settlement houses (cf. Leat, 1975) and industrial training schemes
(cf. Urwick, 1904). All of these attempts at social improvement
and moral regulation were governed by a particular set of fears;
in essence, how to counter the perceived threats of disorder and
degeneration said to be represented by the young unemployed.

In a wider sense, the notion of a 'lost' generation was also
held to compromise the very supremacy of the British race. The
maintenance of empire, the struggle for industrial efficiency, the
creation of a fit and trustworthy urban populace - how could any
of these things be achieved if so many youthful embodiments of
the national character and well-being, lacked loyalty, discipline
and a decent place in the social order. How could youth without
work and poorly educated be expected to serve as faithful and honest
retainers in the forward march of the Great British Family?

There were two profound consequences of successive panics throughout the nineteenth and early twentieth centuries about the condition
of youth which have a decidedly contemporary ring about them. The

first was the package of measures designed to defuse threats, real and imagined, posed by workless youth, e.g. make-work schemes, training schools and increased welfare provision. Second, the steady emergence of the state – at both the national and local levels – as the vehicle for delivering the new provision; a development which in turn confirmed the view that the management and control of the 'youth problem' was too important to be left in private hands (the family) or with voluntary associations (like the boys' clubs set up at the end of the nineteenth century, or those 'model' youth movements such as the boy scouts which emerged at the beginning of the twentieth).

Yet in all this, the British were spared one fear which became manifest in Europe from time to time, namely that of unemployed educated young men. The problem of a surplus young graduate and professional class was frequently a calculation in the thinking of European governments (cf. O'Boyle, 1970), where the most expedient solutions were either to encourage emigration, or to absorb the excess in the expanding state administrative and regulatory agencies. The idea that unemployed graduates would provide an especially difficult stratum was one which has never troubled governments in Britain until fairly recently – a point we take up again at the end of this paper – while the reasons why the British experience has traditionally been so different in this respect, have been convincingly argued by Ben-David (1963-4).

The imagery, then, of workless youth in fairly recent British history has largely crystallised around the (in part contradictory) elements of their supposed demoralisation, capacity for insurrection and irresponsibility, and as a prey for agitators and extremist political Svengalis of every type. Interestingly enough in this context, neither the labour party since its inception nor any of the powerful trade unions have made any serious attempts to organise substantial youth wings and have certainly made no effort to mobilise the young unemployed.

In the next section we turn to some contemporary preoccupations with workless youth, and in particular note how what are regarded as specifically modern concerns and reactions have, in fact, some very long roots. The fears which feed an accumulation of panics about the unemployed young have been carried over time, so that the ancient and the modern become juxtaposed, each drawing upon that peculiar pathology of sentiment about the nature of the problem of workless youth in British society.

CONTEMPORARY OBSESSIONS; WORKLESS YOUTH AS AN 'UNEXPLODED TIME BOMB'

A scattering of newspaper and journal headlines reveals the content of the current panics about the youthful unemployed. '100,000 a year join "time bomb of young jobless" Professor warns' ('Guardian', 10 July 1980); 'Scourge of youth unemployment forces blacks into crime' ('Guardian', 27 July 1980); 'Unemployed a "social time bomb"' ('Guardian', 10 August 1980); '"Mass Revolt" warning by union chief' ('Daily Telegraph', 28 August 1980); 'Jobless riot warning as recession bites deeper' ('Western Mail', 10 September

1980);   'Jobless young turning to crime' ('Guardian', 1 October
1980);   'Crime rise warning' ('South Wales Echo', 30 October 1980)
where, in a typically sombre picture, the National Association for
the Care and Protection of Offenders in its annual report warned
that the growing number of young jobless 'could result' in an
'enormous' rise in crime. Accompanying the fear of unemployment
pushing youth into rebellion and in the direction of more specific
forms of anti-social behaviour such as crime, were broodings about
the alleged impact of unemployment upon the morals and social sensibilities of the young people involved. This was more than the old
scare concerning the supposed link between crime and the workless.
Thus 'More young jobless threaten suicide' ('Guardian', 12 August
1980);   'Women and the great pill debate' ('Western Mail', 26
August 1980);   'Job loss "causing family violence"' ('Guardian',
23 July 1980);   'The jobless teenagers who turn to Vice' ('Western
Mail', 17 December 1980).

The spectres here are ones woven around the supposed widespread
moral and social demoralisation and degeneration among workless
youth, with the principal manifestations said to be the tendencies
towards self-destruction (suicide), the destruction of others (rising intra-family violence), self-degradation (turning to prostitu-
tion 'rather than face the hopelessness of life as a long-term unemployment statistic', 'Western Mail', 17 December 1980), and the
collapse of a positive self-identity which only regular and satisfying work can bring. On this last point a spokesperson for the
Family Planning Association felt able to declare:

If you are involved in a job which brings rewards and satisfactions you are less likely to get into a relationship which
you don't really want. You have something to occupy you and
the self-confidence to say 'No' to boys. It requires some self-
confidence and self-respect to arrange contraception. Those are
qualities which are undermined if you are an unemployed school-
leaver, depressed at being stuck at home with parents who might
be getting at you ('Western Mail', 26 August 1980).

These then are some of the contours of the contemporary concern
about the social, moral and political implications of long-term
youth unemployment. The idea of the young workless as some sort of
delayed high explosive device attached to the hull of the ship of
state has been a favourite theme of recent commentators on the
state of the nation. The leader of the National Union of Mine
Workers warned of how anger over unemployment could erupt into
civil disobedience and a breakdown of public order. His is the
vision of the apocalypse: 'Anybody who looks at the political
scene today with 2,100,000 unemployed can smell it coming. It will
be a conflagration never before seen in this country. The 1926
General Strike was completely different' ('Western Mail', 11
November 1980).

In a similar style, the Director of the EEC Social Affairs Commission predicted that the rising number of unemployed young people
in Europe represented a 'social time-bomb that could explode at
any time' ('Guardian', 10 August 1980). The same scare also sur-
faced in the First Report from the Committee on Welsh Affairs which
placed heavy stress upon the role of unemployment as a prime mover
in creating disorder and mass protest. Here again, the workless

young were adjudged to be especially significant as a potential
catalyst for misrule: 'We are impressed by the conviction of some
of our witnesses who stress the risks of serious social disorder
if there were to be very high and chronic levels of unemployment,
particularly amongst the young' (1980, p.xvii).

What is of special interest about the sweep of these concerns
is not only the belief that unemployment - and particularly the
young unemployed - would trigger dangerous social tensions, there
was also the feeling that the latterday unemployed would never
tolerate the levels of privation borne stoically by previous generations of workless. As the Welsh Affairs Committee put it: 'Wales,
if condemned to suffer the incidence of worklessness endured in the
Thirties, is unlikely to respond with the apathy and despair that
enveloped so many in those days' (1980, p.xvii).

In noting the quiescence of previous generations, the Committee
offers a useful corrective to that tendency to exaggerate the in-
surrectionary potential of the workless. There is little justification for reading British history in this way, a point we take up
in more detail in the next section.

More immediately, modern panics over the young workless have
thrown up a package of make-work schemes sustained by massive
government investment. The special interest in the fate of the
young unemployed has its roots in anxieties over the long term
'psychological' effects on those involved. As Sir Raymond Pennock,
President of the Confederation of British Industries put it:

In the 1930's those who were most bitter, those with the chip
on the shoulder, those who were usually looking for trouble,
were those who had stood in the dole queue and had never for-
gotten it. Unemployment bites deeply, but bites especially
with the young ('The Times', 11 November 1980).

What Pennock gives expression to here is the fear of losing the
loyalty of an unemployed class, even when members of that class
eventually found work. Unemployment, according to this view, scars
those affected by it, and in particular seriously disfigures the
young - thereby producing a stratum whose support for any future
social order will always be suspect. Sentiments of this kind -
which help generate youth job programmes - would seem to provide
partial confirmation of Huston's argument that make-work schemes
'are much more a response to social instability than to an economic
crisis as such' (1972, p.52). Certainly in the short run the simple
existence of unemployment does not threaten capitalist society, and
at times can be useful as a prop in any conservative rule of piety
and iron; but large-scale and long-term unemployment is said to
have a different character. According to this thesis, it is this
which helps undermine the work ethic, and makes difficult the stable
reproduction of a reliable and 'integrated' labour force. But the
difficulty with this formulation lies with the fact that there is
no evidence to suggest that contemporary advanced capitalist
societies (like Britain) are unable to absorb high levels of unemployment, whether it be young people or anybody else. In the next
section we attempt to calculate more precisely just what threat
workless youth do pose to the social fabric. And we begin there
by considering the question - why, in spite of all the forebodings
about the alleged disruptive and cataclysmic effects of youth

unemployment on 'society', are the actual outcomes so apparently
muted and passive? Has 'youth' been misunderstood; or is it more
accurate to say that traditional and popular ways of presenting
the 'youth problem' have been ill-conceived? And is it also possible that contemporary social realities make a nonsense of the
supposed substantive content of recent panics and obsessions about
workless youth being poised to march to war?

'MORAL PANICS' AND SOCIAL REALITIES

The complaint is often made that we wear our history too lightly
and complacently. Social conflicts, political tensions, rebellion
and resistance are all said to have been played down in standard
accounts of social change and process in Britain. A recent paper
by Hart offers some typical complaints against rendering the past
in terms which are too Whiggish and too timid: 'The key concepts
in this view of our history are gradualism, tolerance, adaptation,
evolution and integration' (1980, p.401).
    The implications of these sorts of remarks are clear. Our his-
tory has been more violent and disturbed than we have 'commonly'
supposed, and there is consequently a need for considerations of
trouble and disorder to be given a more central place in discussions on social change. While these strictures are a useful corrective to simple Whig interpretations of history, there are another set of errors which stem from the opposite inclination to read
the past through red-tinted spectacles. The refusal in some quarters to write history through Hart's 'key concepts' has meant a
tendency to generate a set of dramatic histories where the organ-
ising themes are ones of dissent, rebellion and discontent. Discussions of youth have been especially badly served in this respect,
the more so once it is realised that there is almost no evidence to
sustain the view that youth are major carriers of riotous thoughts
and deeds. Perhaps we can make this point best with reference to
the attitudes and behaviour of the workless in general, and the
young unemployed in particular, during the inter-war depression.
The best purgative for those who persist in panicking about the
young workless, is surely the numbing acquiescence of the 'unwaged'
in this period. We know of the General Strike and of 'hunger
marches', but the sum of organised and unorganised troubles were
miniscule when compared to the total unemployed. And within this
theatre of passivity, the young workless were as inconspicuous as
any. Typical here is Jennings's (1934) findings after studying
Brynmawr, a chronically distressed area of South Wales in the 1920s
and 1930s. Her picture was not one of widespread agitation, or of
sights and sounds of an angry and uncompromising youth, but one of
general apathy and drift. At the same time, there was no shortage
of dire predictions as to the consequences of unemployment: 'Enforced idleness leads ultimately ... to envy of those better placed
in society, and envy leads to hatred as hatred leads in the last
resort to social conflict' (Meara, 1936, p.11). But pinning down
the precise moment of the 'last resort' has never proved possible.
Jennings's realities were always to temper the visions and revela-
tions of those like Meara.

Certainly in contemporary times, the brute facts seem to be that workless youth are not a 'problem' in any potentially insurrection-ary sense. There are modern-day spectres to haunt those who are endlessly apprehensive about the condition of youth, but these have nothing at all to do (if they ever did) with the notion of an un-differentiated mob of young workless. 'Youth troubles' today come in more specific packages, with two especially prominent. The first of these relates to racial conflicts. Events at Notting Hill (1976; 1977), Lewisham (1977), Southall (1978), Manchester (1979) and most recently Bristol (1980) were largely built around the activities of young, disaffected males. While the particulars on this list of racial conflicts vary, there are important generalisations we may draw from them. To begin with, there is the way in which unemploy-ment among young blacks has helped fuel wider racial tensions. At the same time, when unemployed young whites have been moved to direct action, they have tended to focus their anger and sourness on various non-white minority groups (cf. Pearson, 1976). The apparent, if localised, success of the National Front and the Brit-ish Movement in attracting support from this disaffected segment of white youth has also been commented upon (cf. Robins and Cohen, 1978; Miles and Phizacklea, 1978), with the point frequently being made that if these impulses go unchecked, they will inevitably lead to a more general and more poisonous contamination.

These points of tension between factions of white and black youth lead into the second area of youth troubles, and once again we find no hint of any broader conflagration in the wind. Rather, what we are referring to here are intra-class conflicts where segments of working-class youth (invariably male) have periodically turned their anger and impatience not onto 'society', but against themselves. Where these fairly minor (if nasty) dramas and confrontations have been acted out (as between, say, punks and teds, or skins and greasers, or even in the more prosaic form of simple gang disputes), although workless youth have loomed large in them the fact of un-employment was and is never a point of struggle and conflict. 'So-ciety' is not put at risk. Thus even though the fact of the parti-cipants being without work may be a contributing ingredient in these tiny eruptions (generating boredom, aggravation and time to burn) the disputes themselves are displaced into other forms.

Certainly contemporary attempts to mobilise the young workless have been either ineptly done, or have failed to have any major appeal, or have not been attempted at all. In the first category we can include the well-meant but extraordinarily naive efforts by the young socialists in the 1960s to carve a constituency out of the disaffected young. One attempt by the Socialist Labour League to mobilise young people - under the banner of 'Mods and Rockers Must Unite to Kick Out the Tories' - was a typically woeful experiment in politicisation. The largely unsuccessful struggles to orches-trate a powerful 'Right to Work' campaign is testimony to the second kind of failure to tap the energies and loyalties of workless youth (indeed, the unemployed generally). The campaign's 300 mile march from South Wales (a jobless blackspot) to the Conservative Party Conference at Brighton (a trek which started on 25 September 1980) failed to tap any general support, or even to attract much interest nationally. The march ended in Brighton with no more recruits than

the 200 who originally set out and most of those were members of
the Socialist Workers' Party ('Western Mail', 10 September 1980;
'Guardian', 9 September 1980). In trying to use the hunger marches
of the 1930s as a point of inspiration, the organisers were playing
a much weaker card than they suspected. The original marches were
never mass mobilisations; then, as now, it was difficult to link
the unemployed and the employed; then, as now, high levels of unemployment could be 'managed' without serious damage to the social
fabric (if we measure this purely in terms of low levels of civil
and political disorder and agitation).

Finally, the trade unions and the Labour party while thundering
against joblessness, and making a special rhetorical pitch over
the young workless, have so far done little or nothing to organise
unemployed workers of any age. This point was at least acknowledged at the last (1980) Trades Union Congress, but as yet with
no solidly tangible consequences. Indeed, the passivity and con-
fusion of the leadership of the Labour party and of organised
labour in conditions of rising unemployment point to the emascu-
lating effect of high levels of joblessness rather than to any
supposed eruptive qualities it might have. In the context of this
inertia - which is partly fuelled by fear and partly by an inability
to organise around alternative programmes - the young unemployed
are quietly buried away. A target, as we have seen, for moralists,
but only a minor irritant on the social body. Protests specifically by jobless youth are rare and even these sporadic actions
have been organised around the narrowest demands for work and not
linked to any wider agitation. Thus limited actions of this kind,
such as the occupation of an empty local authority building in
Brighton by 50 unemployed teenagers ('South Wales Echo', 27 August
1980) are - quite understandably - only an appeal for work and not
a harbinger of general disorder.

In other words, moral panics about the young jobless are well
wide of the mark. Youth's quiescence is merely a part of a much
broader paralysis of a labour force confronted both by rising unemployment and by a government which has been unwilling to grant
to the leadership of labour any serious say in the business of the
regulation of the economy. And in so far as youth raises its voice
at all, the cry is for jobs, for incorporation; their concern is
not to subvert a social order, but to join it.

CONCLUSION

We have tried to show how the problem of youth unemployed is, in
a sense, a thing of no substance. This, of course, is not meant
to imply that workless youth are to be disregarded, but rather to
underline the emptiness of all those fears about the jobless young
as a potential 'great havoc'. At the same time we also indicated
that there are spectres, but that these have nothing to do with the
old - and usually unrealised - fear of undifferentiated mobs of
rootless, urban young pressing hard against the defenders of good
order. Whatever threats are posed by elements of contemporary
youth are highly specific and partial ones. We have seen how local
segments of disaffected black youth have, from time to time, pro-

vided a rebellious core. Again, the tangle of youth unemployment
and racial politics have thrown up other localised points of
friction and conflict. The success 'enjoyed' by the National Front
and the British Movement in tapping currents of racism and xeno-
phobia among sections of white working class youth, are well enough
known now (cf. Pearson, 1975; Miles and Phizacklea, 1978; Seabrook,
1973). Yet even these outbursts and entanglements probably have no
wider social significance. A recent attempt by Ridley to explain
these and other youthful configurations seems close to the mark. In
considering the popular argument that political forces of the extreme left and right were taking full advantage of unemployment, and
of the young jobless especially, Ridley has this to say:

> Whether exclusion from work and rejection by organised society ...
> will lead to serious political alienation is another matter....
> What we may have among the disadvantaged inner city young ... is
> passive alienation. They have opted out of the polity if, in-
> deed, they were ever socialised into it in the first place. There
> is no sign yet of significant political activity among the young
> directed against the existing order. Opinions differ about the
> extent to which alienated youngsters form a pool which could be
> mobilised by political activists. Conservatives and social
> democrats may fear it, the far left may hope for it, but I have
> my doubts. The intellectual demands revolutionary movements
> make on their members (reading news sheets, etc.) and the com-
> mitments of time they demand (selling news sheets, etc.) are
> probably too high. The National Front is another matter, be-
> cause it offers a rather different outlet for frustrated ener-
> gies. Street fights are more likely to strike a chord than
> organised political action. But it is well to remember that
> riots can be triggered off by all sorts of organisations or,
> indeed, by no organisation at all. There, perhaps, lies the
> real danger. A generation idle and frustrated because unem-
> ployed; rejected by employers, thus alienated; concentrated
> in certain districts where the environment itself is grim - not
> revolution, but simple undirected violence and pointless des-
> truction (1981, p.26).

His remarks seem to correspond closely to what we know already
concerning the detail of youthful behaviour, in contrast to wilder
talk about political agitation, social time bombs and the like. In
historical terms the workless young have never been able to dis-
charge the revolutionary load laid upon them, and there is nothing
in the present circumstances to suggest that 'youth' is at last
ready to indulge the hopes of political activists or the fears of
those who, at a distance, imagine every kind of convulsion and
youthful infamy.

To engage for a moment in the sort of speculations which have
characterised so many pronouncements about youth unemployment, it
might perhaps be more profitable to dwell upon the possible long-
term social and political consequences of an un- or under-employed
graduate stratum. It was earlier pointed out that Britain, unlike
most other European countries, had always managed to avoid creating
a surplus 'professional class'. But in circumstances where we are
witnessing a still expanding system of higher education sitting
astride a stagnant or even declining economy, there may well be a

substantial new group of militant young unemployed in the making.
Thus while in the short run the multiplication of educational institutions (along with a lengthening of the period of compulsory
schooling) helps to absorb surplus youth in a fairly comfortable
incarceration, the emergence of members of a large 'educational
class' in a contracting labour market, where there are fewer and
fewer jobs to match their skills and expectations, may be a source
of serious instability.

But more immediately, the idea of the young workless as a troubling issue in the sense intended by those who talk the language of
moral panics is highly fanciful. Political groups have made little
or no headway with this constituency and the trade union movement
has offered few initiatives. While it is true that the Trades
Union Congress sponsored a conference in November 1980 on 'Services
for the Unemployed', their attempt to keep the unemployed within the
embrace of the trade unions has made only limited progress. Moreover, it is likely that the TUC's concern has as much to do with
political fears (the reluctance to see any rival body flourish,
like the inter-war National Unemployed Workers' Movement), as it
has with any clear-cut commitment to the workless.

That the government's efforts to make 'provision' for the young
unemployed are widely regarded as not much more than expensive and
often irrelevant palliatives does not mean that a burgeoning number
of workless youth is any serious threat to 'society'. Perhaps in
the end, moral panics about workless youth tell us far more about
those who fall into a frenzy than it does about the social character
and disposition of the young unemployed. The young remain as they
have always been in contemporary Britain; a battleground for moralists and soothsayers but having, for themselves, precious little
power and leverage on the social system.

Chapter 4

WHOSE NEEDS? SCHOOLING AND THE 'NEEDS' OF INDUSTRY

Dan Finn

Anyone who saw the Tory election poster in 1979 entitled 'Educashun isn't Wurking', with its picture of the dole queue, will have recognised what were by then familiar themes – apart from the recurring faces of Saatchi and Saatchi employees – principally that the poster represented a high point in a campaign which ascribed much of the blame for numerous social and economic problems, particularly those associated with youth unemployment, onto the state sector of education.

From the heyday of educational consensus and expansion in the 1960s, when the new comprehensive schools were proclaimed as the cauldrons within which would be forged the classless workers and citizens of the 'white-hot' technological revolution, we had progressed to a situation where these same schools were popularly portrayed as 'concrete jungles', undermined by subversive teachers and progressive teaching methods, which were producing illiterate and innumerate young workers who could not get jobs. From the first faltering steps of the Black Papers in 1969 (Cox and Dyson, 1969a; 1969b; 1970), the new right had succeeded in shifting the whole terrain of the debate about educational means and ends.

A key component in this debate, and in the policy initiatives which followed, had been a vociferous contribution from employers about schooling's inability to meet their requirements, such that the focus of responses to youth unemployment has been upon the training and education of young workers, rather than the structure and nature of the labour market for young people.

In this chapter, we want to examine this process in more depth, especially as it is these 'needs' of employers which have structured the forms of provision examined in more detail in the other contributions to this collection. Initially, we want to examine more closely what are referred to as the 'needs' of industry. We will then go on to examine the period of the great debate on education. Specifically, we want to argue that the restructuring and transformation of education and training initiated by the last Labour government and largely carried through under the aegis of the Manpower Services Commission derived much of its direction from a politically specific definition of the 'needs' of industry.

Finally, we want to argue that the debate about schools, training and the 'needs' of industry is necessarily political, and that the current debate poses fundamental questions for all of us involved in this area of work.[1]

THE 'NEEDS' OF INDUSTRY

The suggestion that there is a relationship between the education system and the economy has been a core assumption in all the debates about compulsory schooling. Indeed the history of such debates reveals a continuous concern with the quality of labour power. Visions of the perfect worker are ever present - from the frugal and grateful cottagers of the late eighteenth century, through the self-respecting mechanics of the mid-nineteenth and the militaristically marshalled massed workers of the 1890s to the modern subjects of the MSC, complete with 'employability' and 'social and life' skills (see chapters 2 and 9).

In many ways it has been in response to perceived economic problems and the needs of industry - particularly those 'needs' concerned with the quality of workers - that many educational reforms have been precipitated. Similarly, the growth and development of many areas of educational provision, as in further education, have been directly influenced by the activities and demands of employers.

It is not possible, then, to understand the nature and pattern of British educational provision without examining its relationship to the 'needs' of employers. However, this is not to suggest that schools simply prepare their pupils for particular jobs in the labour market. Whilst British education has characteristically been class specific, even within these hierarchies the nature and extent of the relationship between education and employment has been a source of continual controversy and, indeed, the distinction between education and vocational training has been a marked feature of British education.

Whilst education has been most commonly defined as a preparation for life, the emphasis within that definition on the importance of preparation for work has varied historically. Educational policy, for example, also has to deal with the demands of parents and the requirements of future families. Children must be regarded as future parents as well as producers. In other words, education has been the object of other, sometimes contradictory, definitions: it is charged with the task not only of preparing the future workforce, but also with preparing the next generation of citizens, the next generation of parents and so on.

Furthermore, the working class and other subordinate social groupings have struggled over the nature and institutional form of that schooling, so that the present framework of education can in no way been seen simply to express the direct and unproblematic interests of finance and industrial capital. Indeed, if we go back to the 'Fisher Act' of 1918 - which advocated part-time education for all 15- to 18-year-old workers, a proposal successfully resisted by employers - we find that these proposals and their subsequent take up in Labour party policy were articulated against the interests

of industry and employers. It was Tawney's purpose (as the archi-
tect of Labour's pre-war educational policy) to rescue the children
from the clutches of employers, and to define an education against
the demands of employment.

It would be erroneous, then, simply to define the work of schools
as producing factory fodder; they do quite clearly have some autonomy from the needs of employers. Particularly in the post-war
period, schools have not been expected solely to prepare children
for work, and their subjects and teaching have been understood as
indirect preparations for work.

Moreover, it is important not to take employers' statements of
their needs as self-evident. Indeed, it is clear that their 'needs'
can be contradictory, confused or simply unknown. As, for example,
a 'Think-Tank' report observed, even though carrying out its review
of education, training and industrial performance from a single
point of view - 'the "needs" of the world of work' - they discovered
that:

> There are quite serious difficulties about interpreting what
> the needs of industry are.... These (needs) are far from uni-
> form; there are inconsistencies between what employers say they
> want and the values implicit in their selection process; their
> conception of their needs, present and future, is frequently
> not explicit and clearly formulated (Central Policy Review
> Staff, 1980, p.7).

Similarly, it is also necessary to distinguish between different
industrial interests and between industrial and other sectoral
interests. It is not so much a question of the needs of employers
as the logics of capitals. A very different educational logic will
attach to businesses with a high ratio of technically or commercially skilled labour - say the banking or computer-making industries - to capitals which have found a way of exploiting casual
labour by, for example, a reversion to domestic outwork. The former represents educational requirements at their most advanced,
the second an extension of nineteenth-century modes of exploitation which were crudely anti-educational in their effects. Yet
both forms coexist in one society and under the same state.

Further, whilst many employers may require certain definable
technical and scientific skills in their labour force at any given
time, the range and pace of innovation and change in modern labour
processes can soon make these skills redundant. That is to say,
given the nature of contemporary employment, it is clear that employers have a particular interest in minimising their training
costs and gearing it to their own specific and immediate requirements - the training needs to be as brief as possible for a job
which is likely to disappear in a short space of time. What they
require, then, are, for example, skilled workers with the flexibility, adaptability and discipline which enable them to be quickly
trained and retrained for specific jobs over relatively short periods of time.

Thus, there is a real sense in which employers cannot know what
particular technical skills they require from their workers' general education and training - indeed many employers and further
education teachers recognise the technical irrelevance of much of
the content of their curricula for apprenticeships (Gleeson and

Mardle, 1980, chs 3 and 6). They are more concerned with the
general, social dispositions and characteristics of their workers
than with their particular abilities to carry out specific technical tasks. Hence, their demands are usually extremely vague, calling, for example, for a 'sophisticated and flexible labour force',
for workers with the ability to 'learn to learn' and to 'adapt to
change'.

What are articulated as the needs of industry, then, are never
a straightforward or unproblematic expression of the 'objective'
requirements of the labour process. Crucially, the translation of
those 'needs' into a coherent set of demands on the state, and their
resolution in certain policies, is necessarily a political process,
and therefore involves wider issues than the simple representation
of 'objective' problems encountered by employers. In so far as
the skill requirements and technical needs of the economy do mould
the education system, the actual pattern of the influence is necessarily mediated through political and economic ideologies and the
concrete practices and interests of the social groups concerned.

In the 1960s, within the assumptions of the period of educational
consensus, this relationship between school and work appeared to be
largely unproblematic.[2] The organisational structure of schooling
was changed in successive attempts to provide more people, particularly within the working class, with an education which politicians, economists and sociologists regarded without question as a
'good' thing. Even when it was argued, as in the Newsom Report,
that the 'less able' would require a more 'relevant' curriculum,
the emphasis was on education in opposition to training (Central
Advisory Council for Education, 1963, paras 100-16).

It was assumed that the interests of both working-class children
and employers could be met by a massive expansion of educational
provision and by comprehensive reorganisation. The stress on child-
centred education, on classroom flexibility and on developing 'relevant' curricula stemmed from the theory that a vast untapped pool
of ability existed among working-class youngsters and this ability
had to be released to meet both the needs of the economy for more
skilled labour and to provide equal opportunities.

However, with the gradual demise of full employment, the question
of the relatively unstructured relationship between school and work
was to receive increasing political prominence. Similarly, the
accelerating decline of the British economy was to undercut the
assumption of an unproblematic relationship between educational expansion, in its 1960s forms, and economic growth. In effect, the
1960s witnessed a period of the marked autonomy of major sectors of
the education system. In the 1970s, by contrast, massive efforts
were to be made to ensure a closer conformity between the education
system and the necessities of production.

It is important to grasp the nature of the autonomy which we
have used to characterise the schools in the 1960s. We are not
suggesting the absence of a relationship to the economy, but on the
contrary, we are arguing that the particular political and ideological expression of that relationship involved specific forms of
educational reform and expansion, which in turn allowed educational
practices to develop in certain ways. It is this pattern of practices and institutional arrangements, particularly in the schools,
which were to come under attack in the 1970s.

EDUCATION AND WORKING LIFE: THE GREAT DEBATE

The great debate on education initiated by Callaghan at Ruskin
College in October 1976 represented an important transition in the
debate about educational means and ends.   It marked, at the highest
political level, the end of the phase of educational expansion which
had been largely promoted by his own party, and signalled a public
redefinition of educational objectives.

This intervention by the then prime minister not only reflected
an attempt to win political support and secure a new educational
consensus, but it also marked a clear shift on the part of the
Labour leadership into policies which would allow new forms of intervention in the education sector.

Fundamentally, the political initiative to build this new educational settlement was to be constructed around a more direct sub-
ordination of education to what were perceived to be the 'needs' of
the economy and the then government's industrial strategy.   As the
subsequent Green Paper made the point:

It is vital to Britain's economic recovery and standard of living
that the performance of manufacturing industry is improved and
that the whole range of government policies, including education,
contribute as much as possible to improving industrial performance and thereby increasing the national wealth (DES, 1977, p.6).

However, this core theme of education's relationship to economic
performance did not attain its prominent position on the agenda of
the great debate as the result of some natural process.   Rather,
it was defined as a central issue within a wider debate about Britain's economic and social problems.   Constructed over a number of
years, and articulated in various reports and media, the consistent
complaints about falling standards, progressive teachers and education's lack of relevance to working life were transformed into a
wide-ranging critique of the 1960s developments.

At the same time, the relationship between the reforms in secondary schooling, the characteristics of young workers, and the nature
of work discipline were highlighted both by the growth in youth
unemployment and by the complaints of employers.   Not only was there
a growing recognition that being a pupil means being subject to a
different pattern of social control, discipline and freedom but, it
was argued, because of developments within schooling, this pattern
of control, and its associated dispositions, was actually developing
in contradiction to those characteristics required at work.   As an
MSC Training Services Agency (TSA) document made the point in 1975:

In recent years the social environment in a number of schools,
with more emphasis on personal development and less on formal
instruction, has been diverging from that still encountered in
most work situations, where the need to achieve results in conformity with defined standards and to do so within fixed time
limits call for different patterns of behaviour.   The contrast
is more marked where changes in industrial processes have reduced
the scope for individual action and initiative (MSC TSA, 1975,
p.15).

Furthermore, mounting survey evidence from various investigations
was suggesting a breakdown between the demands of employers and the
characteristics of young workers.   In 1974, for example, a major

survey of employers' reactions to young workers found that they were placing increasing emphasis on 'motivation', coupled with 'the fact that a large minority of unemployed young people seem to have attitudes which, whatever their cause or justification, are not acceptable to employers and act as a hindrance to young people in securing jobs' (National Youth Employment Council, 1974, p.29).

These changes in the characteristics of young workers, and the implicit criticisms of the education system, were dramatically expressed in the period preceding the great debate. Particularly important, and in a marked break from post-war practice, some of the major contributions to this critique of the schools were from representatives of industrial capital. Given massive prominence in the media, the criticisms of Sir Arnold Weinstock (managing director, GEC), Sir John Methven (director general of the CBI), Sir Arthur Bryant (head of Wedgewood Pottery), and others consistently portrayed unaccountable teachers teaching an irrelevant curriculum to young workers who were poorly motivated, 'over aspirated', illiterate and innumerate.

It was during this period therefore that discussion of the social purposes of education, and the failings of schooling in particular, became part of the public political discourse. By the time of Callaghan's speech, rather than there being a loose fit between school and work, it had become commonly asserted, amongst other things, that there was a mismatch: 'Some schools may have over-emphasised the importance of preparing boys and girls for their roles in society compared with the need to prepare them for their economic roles' ('Times Educational Supplement', 1976). Similarly, teachers were ignorant about the world of work and were both directing their pupils into the wrong subject areas – too much arts and humanities – and were prejudicing them against industrial employment.

More fundamentally, though, the schools were failing to transmit the necessary basic skills: 'I am concerned ... to find complaints from industry that new recruits from the schools sometimes do not have the basic tools to do the job' (ibid.) and this was swelling the ranks of the young unemployed: 'There is no virtue in producing socially well adjusted members of society who are unemployed because they do not have the skills' (ibid.).

The confident assumption of the 1960s that expanding education would contribute to economic growth had been transformed into the view that many aspects of the education system actively inhibited the profitability and growth of industry.

In this period there was a dual process at work. Not only were the aims and objects of education being redefined, but, at the same time, the actual processes of the education system were being restructured both to achieve these new goals and to fit the new patterns of reduced state expenditure. However, this restructuring of the social relations of schooling was necessarily a long term process and in the meantime massive youth unemployment meant that the need to ensure a disciplined, productive and malleable labour force, or, as the MSC's Holland Report puts it, 'building a workforce better adapted to the needs of the 1980s' (MSC, 1977a, p.7) was too important to be left to the vagaries of the labour market and the streets, or in the hands of an unreformed and 'suspect' educational

apparatus.   It is in this context that we have to see the rise to
power of what has been called 'manpower servicedom'.

THE MSC AND THE DES

Rather than go into the details of the evolution of the MSC and
its training programmes (which are being assessed in another chapter in this collection) we want here to focus on those developments
most directly impinging on education and, more centrally, why it
seems that the education sector is bypassed in the state's response
to youth unemployment.

   In the first instance, the MSC, through the TSA, initiated a
debate about the vocational preparation of young people in 1975
which subsequently was to become a key mechanism for redefining
the relationship between education and training (MSC TSA, 1975).
On a practical level, the most important development concerned
both the expansion of the Training Opportunities Programme (TOPS)
and its relative shift in location from the TSA's own skill centres
to colleges of further education.

   In the early 1970s the DES was subjected to two official investigations - by the OECD and the House of Commons Public Expenditure
Committee - both of which were critical of the DES's role in policy
making. More importantly, however, during the proceedings of the
Public Expenditure Committee it became apparent that far from dic-
tating policy, the DES was significantly hamstrung in its activities.
Central policies had to be translated into practice via the financial
and political autonomy of local education authorities, and, as with
Tameside's refusal to go comprehensive, this decentralised power
structure posed acute problems for any national initiatives emanating
from the DES.

   Furthermore, it became apparent in the evidence of the MSC that
the DES had lost the initiative in responding to youth unemployment,
and that the integration of training and further education was pro-
ceeding on the terms dictated by the TSA: 'it would be true to say
that in recent times much of the initiative in terms of new plans
and progress has come from our side of the fence rather than theirs'
(House of Commons Public Expenditure Committee, 1976, p.238). Similarly, these policy initiatives were, at the ground-floor level,
transforming the work of the colleges: 'it is a fact that we have
been expanding our training activities ... much more rapidly than
educational activity has been expanding' (ibid., p.240). As NATFHE
argued in their evidence, the TSA was posing 'fundamental issues of
educational principle'. The Public Expenditure Committee concluded
from the evidence that the 'DES and the Department of Employment
are in a sense competing for resources and liable to be judged one
against the other by result.' The DES was thought to be 'less
nimble in a situation where objectives themselves are changing'
than in more routine matters, and the TSA 'has moved at a tempo
which DES could not (and indeed should not try to) emulate.' The
Committee welcomed 'the initiative and enthusiasm displayed by the
TSA' (ibid., p.xxviii).

   It is in this context that we have to see the rise to power of
the MSC. Unfettered by the political and financial constraints of

the education sector, and more ideologically in tune with the then government's industrial strategy, the MSC was able to take initiatives and make proposals thereby 'winning' this whole area of institutional expansion.

Nowhere was this more apparent than in the debate the TSA initiated on the vocational preparation of young people. While the specific programme advocated by Labour has been rejected by the Conservatives and the CBI - the pilot programmes are continuing - the underlying importance of this debate came through its redefinition of the relationship between education and training. For example, in the government consultative paper on policy for the 16- to 18-year age group, we find 'vocational preparation' replacing older definitions:

> the terms 'training' and 'education' have been commonly used as a rough and ready means of distinguishing between learning to perform specific vocational tasks (training) and the general development of knowledge, moral values and understanding required in all walks of life (education). But such definitions have obvious shortcomings.... The concept of vocational preparation treats the entire process of learning, on and off the job, as a single entity, combining elements of training and education to be conceived and planned as a whole (DES, 1979, p.10).

So the debate about the inefficiency of schools, and the inadequacy of the training services, to prepare 'youngsters for working life', carried within it a redefinition of the role of these agencies in the reproduction of the labour force. As the proposals for pilot schemes of Unified Vocational Preparation made clear: 'A new relationship will need to be created between the education and training services; and new methods will have to be developed' (DES, 1976, p.3).

YOUTH UNEMPLOYMENT AND THE LABOUR PROCESS

In the crisis of education of the late 1970s we have emphasised two key policy components - the increasing involvement of the state in training, epitomised in the creation of a new training agency, and the increasing pressure on schools to be responsive to the needs of industry. Both these policies have to be understood by reference to the economic recession and, in particular, to the problems of youth employment. Indeed, we cannot understand what is happening in schools, further education colleges, skill centres, etc., without reference to the state's recognition that youth unemployment is a permanent feature of the British economy.

Nevertheless, we cannot simply 'read off' schooling's response from the 'needs' of the labour market as a one-dimensional model of problem and response. Thus, the first response of the Labour government of 1974-9 to the problem of rising youth unemployment was to solve the problem at its source: employers were offered subsidies and financial incentives to recruit school-leavers. The policy did not work because capitalists cannot be forced to employ the young - this is the reality of market power that faces any British government. Employers' reasons for not recruiting school-leavers and their accounts of the needs of industry, therefore, have

to be taken as given. It is for this reason that in political/
policy terms youth unemployment is a youth problem: the state
cannot change the labour process to fit existing school-leavers, it
has to try to fit school-leavers to the available labour process.
The origins of youth unemployment may lie in investment and labour
process policies, but the political solution to youth unemployment
in a capitalist economy can only lie in changing the young themselves. This is why an employment problem is transformed into an
education crisis.

   For the state, the most dramatic problem posed by the young
workless is that of social and political unrest. But the educational problem is employability. The state has to ensure that the
young unemployed will be good workers, whether in general terms of
discipline or specific terms of skills, when they do eventually
get jobs. The immediate consequence of youth unemployment is that
the transition from school to work lasts a long time. School-
leavers no longer get immediate work experience and so schools and
training programmes have to become the source of the work ethic;
the state is held responsible for the processes of work socialisation that used to be a normal part of leaving school and getting
a job. Some of this responsibility is borne by the MSC, but schools
are also expected to put a new emphasis on vocational preparation.

   What is at issue here is not only schools' usual role in the
classification and qualifying of labour, but also a concept of education as a direct preparation for work. Schooling for unemployment involves, paradoxically, more efficient education for employment: it is as if teachers now have to instil the work ethic deeply
enough for it to survive lengthy periods out of work. Schools have
to instruct in attitude as well as skills: in preparing their
pupils for the local labour market they have to prepare them to
accept the available jobs. The stress is on 'realism' - work experience schemes are as important as lessons in Maths and English.
All teachers have to become careers teachers, assessing their subjects and their pupils with reference to local job opportunities.

   The intention is to fit schools and education more firmly into
the set of institutions in which young people are prepared for work.
The traditional distinction between education and training has been
redefined.

   The question we must now address is why has youth been so dramatically affected by the economic crisis. For a number of reasons
school-leavers are having to compete with experienced workers for
jobs in a contracting labour market without any longer having a
market advantage as cheap labour. The problem for the state is
that it is increasingly difficult for inexperienced young workers
to get jobs, but without jobs they cannot get experience.

   Employers' reluctance to employ school-leavers - the immediate
cause of youth unemployment - reflects, at least in part, their
judgment that the qualities they want in their work-force - the
qualities associated with experience - are not those produced by
schooling. Employers are increasingly unwilling to accept that
school success guarantees work success. This is why the 'needs' of
industry, cited in the demands made on schools as a consequence of
youth unemployment, are expressed in terms of a critique of current
educational practice.

This critique has two components. First, schools are blamed
for Britain's shortage of skilled labour. In terms of crafts,
this suggestion is ridiculous. The underlying cause of skill
shortage is, in fact, the trade cycle. The shortage derives from
the contradictions between individual employers' short-term interests and the long-term needs of the economy as a whole. Bad
times for capital means a declining number of apprentices and
trainees - firms have less immediate need for their skills and
less spare cash available for their training. When the economy
picks up, it inevitably does so with a shortage of trained and
skilled workers.

The concept of skill shortage is misleading, and the educational
point actually rests on a distinction between 'general' and 'specific' skills. From the employers' point of view the problem is
not a shortage of craft workers but of a labour force with the
general ability to learn, adapt to change and accept training and
retraining (Blackburn and Mann, 1979, pp.99-109). As a document
on shortages of engineering craftsmen made the point:

> the young person who enters industry today will be required in
> middle or later life to tackle jobs that have little relation
> to jobs as they now exist. A vital quality needed to cope with
> industrial change is adaptability. There is likely to be a
> reduced need in the future of 'skill' in the traditional sense
> but a growing need for 'general mechanical intelligence'
> (National Economic Development Office, 1977, p.23).

What is being demanded from the 'skilled' worker is not a specific
task ability but a general set of attitudes.

The second component of the industrialists' critique of education
is their assertion that school-leavers are ignorant. On the one
hand, school-leavers are believed to be illiterate and innumerate.
On the other hand, it is alleged school-leavers 'don't know what
working life is about': the MSC calls for an improved careers
service, for the 'familiarisation' of teachers with industry; the
Schools Council and CBI set up their own industry project; the DES
(and EEC) are suddenly obsessed with the 'education/work interface'.

However, what is at issue in this second point is not ignorance
but knowledge: what really worries employers is that their young
workers know all to well what their jobs will involve. The problem
is again one of attitudes. In the words of one manager - of Thorn
Electrical - school-leavers are too often 'over aspirated (sic). The
schools do not want to turn out production operatives' (Fryer, 1977).

On closer examination, it turns out that the comments on the
three Rs are also entwined with an argument about attitudes. The
Holland Report links them with simultaneous comments about poor
motivation (MSC, 1977a, p.17), and it is in practice difficult to
separate problems of ability from problems of self-discipline and
application. The criticism of schools for producing 'ignorant'
workers is simultaneously a criticism of schools for producing unwilling workers.

Employers themselves believe that school-leavers are different
from what they used to be, but what is more evident is the change
in labour demand. As Frith (1978a) points out, young workers have
always been characterised as casual, irresponsible, poorly motivated and quick to change jobs. What is new is the employers'

expectation that school-leavers should have the sense of responsibility and commitment that are usually the products of experience. This expectation is partly a result of the availability of such workers, but, more importantly, it also reflects changes in the labour process and changes in the mode of labour control.

Young workers' commitment to work has always been problematic as they have not yet acquired long term family and domestic responsibilities. Their restlessness and readiness to change jobs - their immunity from the stability of long-term instrumentality - have persistently been highlighted. What is novel is not these characteristics, but, in the first place, the availability of adult workers with long-term commitments, and second, the contraction of occupations in which these characteristics do not matter because other forms of labour control operate - for example, in construction.

Previously, many of the unskilled and unqualified young have found work in casual trades where their control depended on direct discipline and supervision - such jobs are now being reorganised. As industry reduces its work-force, there is less spare labour power to provide either on the job training or continuous supervision: firms find it cheaper and more 'rational' to recruit workers who do not need such training or supervision, who are already relatively self-disciplined and reliable. Casual labour is transformed into 'semi-skilled' work.

Similarly, craft skills and apprenticeship training are also being reorganised. One of the functions of apprenticeship is the transmission of craft pride, itself a form of work discipline. But such craft control is being replaced by a different logic of skill, in which skilled workers' discipline rests not on marketable craft qualifications, but on an employer dependent role in a labour hierarchy, on their acceptance of 'responsible autonomy', on their flexible and cooperative attitudes (Blackburn and Mann, 1979, pp.95-100). As Frith concludes:

> Young workers today enter a labour market in which there are fewer and fewer openings for either skilled craftsmen or for unskilled casual labourers. The dominant demand is for generalised, semi-skilled labour power. The shifting employment opportunities resulting from the rise of service occupations, technological changes in production, the decline of small firms mean, too, shifting modes of labour control. It is in this context that the young compete unequally with experienced adults. They lack commitment and discipline and 'realism'. These are the qualities which schools have 'failed' to instil. These are the qualities which have to be instilled by the state, as it takes on responsibility for the now lengthy period of transition from school to work (1978a, p.4).

THE 'CRISIS' IN EDUCATION

We have been arguing that the 'crisis' in education in the 1970s, whilst specific to educational debates and practices, was in large part structured and precipitated by a labour process crisis. The problem became an educational one out of political necessity - the state in a capitalist economy can manipulate education and training

policy directly, it can only change production policies indirectly.
But even this account of the 'crisis' in education is too simple.
The changing needs of industry have their own direct effects on
schooling, and the education 'crisis' was not simply manufactured
by politicians. For school-leavers and their parents the realities
of unemployment are a direct challenge to the legitimacy of schooling.

The 1960s equation of schooling and economic growth had an indi-
vidualistic component: schools presented themselves to their users
as the means to individual mobility. Thus in the 1970s it was not
only employers who felt that schools were failing them; so did
parents. It is an inevitable consequence of meritocratic ideology
that some pupils end up at the bottom of the ladder - their failure
can be blamed on their lack of ability - but the social democratic
version of meritocracy stressed schools' ability to better pupils
regardless of their aptitudes. It was this claim that in the 1970s
became increasingly empty, both for the large numbers of pupils who
continued to leave school without any qualifications and for those
who found that their school achievements had no value in the labour
market.

It was in this context that ideological attacks on social democratic education had political resonance. Since 1945 the political
consensus had been that the central purpose of education was to extend individual opportunity; the debates focused on school organisation rather than on school content. The control of education
seemed unproblematic - as everyone was agreed about the purpose of
schools, what happened inside them could be left to teachers' professional expertise. The fit between educational opportunity and
job opportunity was taken for granted. It was this account of education that ceased to make sense, as school-leavers found it increasingly difficult to get a job and were told that they lacked the
necessary skills, qualifications and aptitudes. Their schools were
held to blame, and the new right in the Conservative party (drawing
on and extending the earlier political work of the Black Papers)
began to develop an effective populist critique of educational progress that reinforced the complaints of employers. Youth unemployment, it was argued, was a symptom of a breakdown in schooling;
schools were not doing their job; children were leaving them unable
to read and write; progressive methods meant ignorance and indis-
cipline. Comprehensive schools began to be reported only in terms
of trouble. Media concern shifted from the needs of the educationally deprived to the needs of the 'exceptionally able'.

Such reporting was not just a right-wing media conspiracy. It
reflected too a more general disillusion with the experience of
schooling. For pupils and parents, the problem was not that schools
had become more unpleasant or irrelevant, but that the benefits
promised by the 1960s advocates of reorganisation had not mater-
ialised. The educational debate shifted from questions of organisation and selection to questions of content and control. It was
in this context that the needs of industry were linked to the need
for a core curriculum and nationwide measurement of standards; that
the industrial irrelevance of school curricula was attributed to
teacher autonomy; that schools' new role in work socialisation
was linked to arguments about schools' accountability.

The great debate, then, was not simply manufactured by the state.
Precisely because of the necessary connection between school and
work, any breakdown in the relationship has immediate consequences
for the ideology of schooling. Similarly, the labour process is
not a completely independent variable. The expansion and reorganisation of education in the 1960s did have industrial consequences:
managerial attacks on schools are not purely rhetorical; firms can
document declining standards among their recruits.

The nub of industrialists' educational complaints are that
schools discourage industrial careers, that school-leavers are not
willing to accept industrial discipline. Such complaints are,
paradoxically, a measure of the success of social democratic education. Over the last twenty years it has become easier for able
working-class children to do well at school and to proceed to
higher education; success at school is still measured in academic
terms. Employers are having to recruit their skilled workers, their
apprentices, from pupils who are, in such academic terms, less well
qualified than in previous generations. Similarly, if employers
are correct in saying that school-leavers are becoming less willing
to do what are (by employers' own admission) more and more tedious
tasks, then this is a measure of the success of teachers in giving
their pupils a sense of their potential, an expectation that work -
in industry as at school - should involve some degree of self-
expression or self-fulfilment.

In practice, whether managers' assessment of the extent and
effectiveness of 'progressive' education is true or not is irrelevant. What matters is that in the context of economic decline and
deindustrialisation, their solution to the problem of managing
young workers has been to reorganise the labour process so as substantially to exclude the young altogether.

EDUCATION, POLITICS AND THE 'NEEDS' OF INDUSTRY

The political relationship between education and industry will continue to change. The development of new technologies, to give the
most immediate example, is having a dramatic effect on white-collar
work and thus on the labour market significance of basic school
qualifications in literacy and numeracy. In shops and offices
alike traditional white-collar work will become increasingly a
matter of repeating routine tasks under the 'supervision' of a
machine; white-collar 'training' will be instant on-the-job instruction; white-collar 'skills' will be the ability to adapt to
shifting technological tasks and the willingness to work 'respon-
sibly' with expensive electronic equipment (see, for example, Barker
and Downing, 1980). The problem of relating education and industry
has, then, no permanent solution. New hierarchies and divisions
in the labour process will continue to need new forms of legitimation and preparation in schools and colleges, and there will
always be tensions in the capitalist education process itself,
tensions whose political solutions will be contested.

In fact, a fruitful way of understanding the development of educational policy is as a series of challenges to the legitimacy of
educational outcomes as they exist, and a series of responses that

take the form of the search for a new basis. Legitimations of
various forms of selection and exclusion, for instance, have
shifted from overtly class-based justifications (with separate
types of school for working- and middle-class children), to justifications in terms of naturally existing types of children (whether
defined in terms of intelligence testing or by rules of thumb about
the 'academic', 'technical' and 'practical' child), to justifications in terms of achievement, 'failure' and educational performance. It has been a feature of the post-war situation in Britain,
however, that the legitimacy of educational outcomes has, almost
continuously, been in dispute.

The politics of capitalist education, then, have always revolved
around the problems of class divisions and their legitimation.
Similarly, schools also play an important part in the sexual dif-
ferentiation of labour, in the reproduction and legitimation of the
divisions between domestic and non-domestic workers. The educational
problem is how to relate girls' preparation for the labour market
to their preparation for family life. In the Labour party's 1977
Green Paper (DES, 1977) there was strong emphasis on the need for
girls to have equal opportunities to pursue careers. The Green
Paper even adopted feminist arguments, for example, criticising
the sex typing of school subjects (science for boys, home economics
for girls). The Green Paper pointed out that schools had to respond to the implications of equal-opportunities legislation: girls
and boys had to have equal forms of vocational preparation. And
yet, simultaneously, the Green Paper called for a new approach to
family education, and stressed schools' role in preparing girls for
domestic labour. The hidden implication (even more apparent in
Conservative policy) is that for girls who end up in jobs (rather
than careers) the family is still the central 'vocation'.

In the period we have looked at, employers' definitions of the
needs of industry were prioritised on the educational agenda. The
success of the new right in articulating these demands to their
critique of the 1960s developments and the connection then made
with parental anxieties set both the agenda for the great debate
and appears to have won consent and support from working-class
parents for the restructuring of education and training. Perhaps
this is because, in a period of scarce jobs, working-class parents
are glad to see their children undergoing the process of becoming
skilled even if it is for particular jobs in routine manual labour
or, in many instances, for jobs which are unlikely to exist at all.
Perhaps it is because, if comprehensivisation, in the form in which
it was implemented, and other radical education programmes are not
going after all to deliver the goods for working-class children,
then they may have to be content to be 'skilled' and 'classed' in
a way that seems appropriate (see Hall, 1979).

However, the success of the MSC training programmes in achieving
an uneasy, but fairly successful depoliticisation of youth unemployment (see chapter 6) - through its corporate political and administrative structure - is not so easily reproduced with the schools.
Teachers are, not surprisingly, suspicious of the argument that
equates education with employer accounts of work preparation. This
seems to be a particularly limiting definition of pupils' intellectual abilities and needs - the needs of industry are, in

educational terms, extraordinarily narrow. And this is not just
an educational issue: it also involves a critique of the labour
process itself. Teachers, rightly, want to preserve the energy,
creativity and individuality that the best lessons can encourage
in their pupils, and the real problem is not what happens to these
qualities in schools, but what happens to them afterwards. Most
school-leavers will never express their 'potential' at work, whatever happened to them at school. Industrialists have had no compunction in criticising education in terms of the needs of industry;
educators should have no compunction in criticising industry in
terms of human needs.

Whether this contradiction is made to become the object of
political struggle remains to be seen, but this is undoubtedly the
most important consequence of the debate about schools and industry: it has made explicitly political the central question - what
is education for?

As a final observation on the 'needs' of industry, it might be
worth reflecting on R.H. Tawney's assessment of the Federation of
British Industries' particular conception of education's value,
revealed in its response to the 1918 'Fisher Act':

> its consequences are simple. They are some new form of slavery.
> Stripped of its decent draperies of convention, what it means
> is that education is to be used not to enable human beings to
> become themselves through the development of their personali-
> ties, nor to strengthen the spirit of social solidarity, nor to
> prepare men for the better service of their fellows, nor to
> raise the general level of society; but to create a new com-
> mercial aristocracy, based on the selection for higher education
> of 'the more promising' children of working class parents from
> among the vulgar mass, who are fit only to serve as the cannon
> fodder of capitalist industry (Tawney, 1973, p.255).

NOTES

1 This chapter draws on the collective work of the Conference of
   Socialist Economists Education Group on education and training,
   particularly with Simon Frith, and draws heavily on an unpublished paper presented by him to the group (Frith, 1978a).
2 For an extensive discussion of the politics of education in this
   period see, Centre for Contemporary Cultural Studies Education
   Group (1981).

Chapter 5

WHO CARES? THE MSC INTERVENTIONS: FULL OF EASTER PROMISE

Graham Markall and Denis Gregory

The previous chapter began to trace the effects which the collapse
of ostensible full employment had upon education and training
policy. It explored the impact of changes in labour demand upon
the legitimacy of schooling and highlighted the perpetual uncer-
tainties and uneasy compromises which have characterised the process of schooling in the face of the contradictory demands made
upon it. We have seen in the previous chapter that schools have
been expected to both transmit and regulate knowledge; to promote
'pupil centred' teaching and a common curriculum; to prepare
youngsters for wage and domestic labour; to be cheap and effective; to foster aspiration and accommodation. Crucially, the
appearance of mass unemployment and particularly the disproportionate impact upon school-leavers and young workers (see chapter
1) has exposed what was always only a contingent relationship between the obfuscatory 'progressivism' of former educational pre-
scriptions and the buoyant labour market of the 1950s and 1960s.

Yet it was a relationship which social democratic assumptions
held to be a causal one. Education was a wholly 'good thing' which
'brought its own rewards' and automatically lubricated the easy
progression from the educational to the occupational gradient.
Thus, when 'the transition from school to work' came to signify
something more than a self-evident physical relocation (i.e. a
hazardous, lengthy and debilitating process for many youngsters),
then the supposedly straightforward association between school
and work, between educational achievement and occupational entry,
came to be threatened. More particularly, explanations were needed
and resolutions sought for the 'breakdown' and 'mismatch' in an
apparently intimate relationship. The deepening recession, the
growth of mass unemployment and the rupture of many youngsters'
post-school lives have proved to be the watershed for the hitherto
unremarkable 'transition from school to work' and have seen the
full clamour of the great debate, the assault upon schooling's aims
and achievements, the exposure of the Department of Education and
Science (DES) and, critically, the emergence and rise of the Manpower Services Commission (MSC) at the centre of the latest site
of education and training reform.

Given its scale and rapid rate of growth it is perhaps useful to give a very brief account of the MSC itself as a large and complex institution and, in particular, identify those areas of its multifaceted operation which are of prime importance for the young unemployed.

The MSC was established on 1 January 1974 by the then Conservative administration and is now organised into three main operating divisions: the Employment Services Division (ESD) which administers the job centres, mobility and occupational guidance, professional and executive recruitment and so on; the Training Services Division (TSD), which finances and monitors most of the training schemes; and the Special Programmes Division (SPD), which is largely concerned with provision for the young unemployed and with implementing the Holland Report's (MSC, 1977a) Youth Opportunities Programme (YOP). Its expansion throughout the 1970s has been both swift and extensive. Its budget has grown from around £125 million in 1974 to some £685 million in 1979-80 and from its original small nucleus of civil servants in 1974 it has grown to employ over 25,000 people in 1980 (see MSC, 1980b, pp.31-2) and exercises a direct interest in over 1,000 skillcentres and colleges around the country (for a detailed picture of its organisational structure see MSC, 1980b, figure 1).

Its size and complexity has clearly been reflected in the nature and scale of its operations in the labour market. Until its appearance in the mid-1970s, state intervention in the operation of the labour market had been restricted to a peripheral involvement in orthodox skills training for industry, in counter cyclical attempts to accommodate the perennial complaints of skills shortages from capital and in the direct low level provision of 'sheltered' employment for groups such as the mentally and physically handicapped marginalised by capital's disinclination to employ as long as there were adequate supplies of able bodied (and less costly) labour available. However, as the recession deepened and its effects began to be felt on the unemployment register, the MSC first attempted to alleviate the crisis by introducing a series of unprecedented direct financial subsidies and inducements to capital to salvage and preserve existing jobs. Furthermore, in its first commissioned work the MSC immediately recognised that 'passivity or an appearance of indifference on the part of policy makers to a lot of unemployment lasting for quite some time may be calamitous from both economic and political viewpoints' (Mukherjee, 1974, p.74).

Essentially and to date statutory interventions in the labour market have assumed three forms:
1 direct financial support to employers to retain existing jobs (e.g. Temporary Employment Subsidy);
2 training incentives, grants and awards in an attempt to secure future stocks of orthodox vocational skills (e.g. Apprenticeship Award Scheme);
3 the creation and colonisation of an entirely new site as the source of work socialisation ('work experience') for the thousands of young workers unable to breach the labour market proper (e.g. Job Creation Programme, Youth Opportunities Programme).

It is the last of these three spheres operated by MSC's Special Programme Division which has enjoyed particularly massive central

government funding and which continues to be sheltered from successive rounds of public expenditure cut-backs. Even in 1977 (only
three years after the emergence of MSC itself) its growth had been
so rapid and extensive that the MSC's chairman could claim: 'a
programme on this scale, of such complexity and such comprehensive-
ness is unique in the Western world, and is at the moment on the
agenda of manpower planners throughout Europe and North America'
(O'Brien, 1977).

The previous chapter has already explored the terrain upon which
new political settlements have been struck and the institutional
and ideological purchase which the MSC has enjoyed in favour of a
discredited and suspect DES. The purpose of this chapter is to try
and examine the recent extensive development of the MSC itself and
to identify the interventionist ideology and practice in the current
recession. And if we pursue the central theme of the previous chapter - that the fragile and vulnerable relationship between education,
training and the 'needs' of industry is always and only temporarily
founded upon a process of political struggle and settlement - then
this chapter will necessarily have to extend consideration beyond
the MSC's own early disingenuous claim as merely operating '*to
alleviate the worst effects* of the highest level of unemployment
since the war' (MSC, 1976a, p.2, our emphasis) and consider its
essentially political purpose and impact.

In truth, as it has developed, the MSC has come to proclaim its
own role as more than simply 'fire fighting' and heralded the occa-
sion 'to turn a major problem and cost into an opportunity and a
benefit' (MSC, 1977a, p.7) and to 'build a work-force better adapted
to the needs of the 1980s' (ibid., p.7). Although it will be argued
that even as a hurriedly implemented emergency response to the crisis
in youth unemployment the early 'special measures' were not without
their political resonances, it is perhaps useful to try to examine
separately various interrelated aspects of MSC activity.

First, we will look at the MSC's 'Special Programmes' structurally
and institutionally at the centre of the site of the latest reform
in education and training. For analytical purposes this comprises
an examination of the 'Special Programmes' both as an accommodative
response to the rapid growth of youth unemployment which attempts
to proscribe and restrict response to it and also as a transformative attempt to intervene materially, culturally and ideologically
in the sphere of education and training.[1] Second, in emphasising
the vulnerability of the latest settlement and the need for continuing struggle around it, we will go on to examine the changing
and problematic role and function of the MSC within the continuing
crisis and in relation to macro-economic policy.

AN ACCOMMODATIVE RESPONSE

In the previous chapter we have seen the restructuring of the ideology and practice of schooling which the crisis in 'the transition
from school to work' currently signifies. But what are the critical
cultural, economic, social and political processes encapsulated in
the post-school transition which attract such continuing close attention from the state and from MSC in particular? Why have so many of

the latter's more radical and extensive overtures in the labour
market been made exclusively towards the young unemployed? Currently, for example, the middle-aged unemployed, with decades of
proven commitment and the dependency on wage labour, suffer trau-
matically in the massive shake out of labour. Yet they certainly
do not receive the same extent of provision as their younger counterparts. At the time of writing all 16- to 18-year-olds who have
been unemployed for six weeks are eligible for the 'special measures' whereas 19- to 24-year-olds are eligible only after six
months of continuous unemployment while those over 24 years of age
have to endure a full twelve months of continuous unemployment to
become eligible. Moreover, the unemployed school-leaver benefits
from the MSC's 'Easter promise': a pledge made by the Commission
that by the Easter following their leaving school all unemployed
youngsters will have either been placed or offered a place on a
YOP scheme. Why is it that the young appear to self-evidently
worthy and enjoy such expensive priority in an implicit hierarchy
of the deserving? In one crude sense, of course, and in accordance
with currently prevailing political orthodoxy, they cannot be
'blamed' for their own unemployment in the same way that older
workers are held to be 'losing' jobs with 'excessive' pay demands
and 'restrictive practices'. First-time job seekers in particular
can hardly 'price themselves' out of jobs which they have never
held (though we can see how the 'sins of the fathers' could be
held to have visited upon them or how their own 'unrealistic' expectations conflict with the 'needs' of industry).

Crucially, 'the transition from school to work' signifies more
than a procession of innocents; it represents a critical stage in
the cycle of reproduction of labour power. The transition here is
from the social relations of dependence, which characterise schooling and the family, to the heart of the relations of capitalist
production and consumption. It is the transition from pupil to
worker, from school to wage and/or domestic labour and is always a
fragile and vulnerable one. We have already seen in the previous
chapter that adolescents in the labour market have always been
typified as irresponsible, feckless, etc., and it is that marginal
relationship and the relative independence from the usual sites of
social relations which underscores the massive contemporary (and
historical) concern with adolescence. In the years of ostensible
full employment their restlessness could be indulged as 'growing
up', 'finding their feet', 'choosing a career', etc., and they
could be 'counselled' and 'guided' occupationally in a buoyant
labour market. What was achieved here through the rhetoric of
voluntarism was the stable reproduction of the labour force over
time; the safe recruitment of the young to their role within the
next generation of wage and domestic labourers.

However, if it has formerly been achieved it is always at risk
and currently exposed by the apparent demise of full employment.
Not only must the potential labour force, tomorrow's prime age,
mature workers, be prepared for entry into work but, crucially,
for wage labour within the antagonistic social relations of capi-
talism. This is the kernel of the problem of 'the transition from
school to work' which is currently revealed by mass youth unemployment. Large numbers of young people are expected to nourish the

seeds of a 'work ethic' whilst simultaneously denied access to
work. Youth thus becomes more than a metaphor for restlessness or
ill discipline; it comes to signal the possibility of real social
and political unrest. The British Youth Council has made the point:

> The MSC has indeed declared its fear that the failure of young
> people to get a job may alienate them from the world of work and
> from society. Not only does this bode ill for the future pro-
> ductivity of the country's potential labour force, but it is
> also likely to cause high levels of crime and social unrest
> (British Youth Council, 1977, p.12).

The same fears about unemployed and disaffected youth, voiced
more or less coherently by politicians, national governments, youth
organisations, statutory agencies and industrialists have had widespread publicity. Yet while the interventionist rhetoric of the
'Special Programmes' sought 'to demonstrate by deeds rather than
by words that society cares about them' (MSC, 1977a, p.7), the
problem of mass youth unemployment to which MSC programmes are a
'caring' response are not simply economic (much less moral or ethi-
cal), they are profoundly political and impelled by very real fears
of social and political disruption. In proclaiming 'a programme ...
unique in the western world' Sir Richard O'Brien precisely captured
the central political work of the 'special measures':

> They provide a means whereby we can pursue industrial efficiency
> and competitiveness without individuals suffering unacceptably,
> and so becoming casualties of, or perhaps enemies to the society
> which by failing to give them a chance to work has rejected
> them (O'Brien, 1977).

Thus, fundamental conflicts arising from the pursuit of 'industrial efficiency and competitiveness' and the marginalisation of
its 'casualties' are now immediately precipitated upon and incor-
porated by the state. By assuming a major responsibility in reproducing future generations of labour, by enlarging its sphere of
operations and by promoting apparatuses such as MSC, the state has
come to assume an increasingly central and direct role in the economic management of capital, acting to defuse and mitigate the
social and political consequences of its continuing crisis. In
attempting to understand the nature of MSC as a state apparatus,
it is vital to locate its ideology and practice and identify the
terrain on which central political bargains are struck:

> The Commission can be successful in its endeavours only by
> taking people along with it. In a free society, much the most
> effective way of securing the commitment of organisations and
> people to a course of action is to involve them in decisions,
> and we therefore consider it essential for there to be partici-
> pation of the major interests concerned, and particularly employ-
> ers' organisations and trade unions, in the work of the central
> manpower authority and at many other levels (MSC, 1976b, p.7).

Articulated at the highest rhetorical level through the 'national
interest', the state thus acts as co-ordinator and 'neutral' arbiter
between the 'twin giants' of labour and capital, drawing their cen-
tralised and bureaucratic structures into active collaboration in
pursuit of the consensus. In its attempt at 'taking people along
with it', we have seen that the MSC incorporates trades unionists
and employers (notionally as equal partners) into its central,

regional and local structures, reflecting its strategy of co-opting
organised labour and capital in order to accommodate successfully
particular economic and social strategies. And the political and
ideological success of the state's education, training and manpower
reforms, the means whereby its definitions of the crisis in 'the
transition from school to work' have been largely accepted can only
be explained with reference to the mobilisation of consent; not
least amongst organised labour. In this way the question of mass
youth unemployment, for example, becomes effectively depoliticised.
It becomes a technical/organisational problem requiring endeavour,
commitment and collaboration in the 'national interest' and is most
certainly not a political problem around production for profit and
the free movement of capital. None of this is to deny the constructive and progressive responses to local employment problems that
have been developed through the 'Special Programmes' in certain
areas (often through or in cooperation with organised labour and
its representatives) but nevertheless it is only by grasping the
wider point that we can begin to appreciate the terrain on which
alternative policies and definitions must struggle.

It is at this point that we can see that the MSC cannot simply
be understood as a palliative to unemployment, nor can it intervene
unequivocally in the 'best interests' of all but rather that it is
a key apparatus in a long term political strategy to restructure
production. But, essentially, it will not do so by reorganising
or controlling capital but rather by the recomposition of labour
('a chance to build a work-force better adapted to the needs of
the 1980s', MSC, 1977a, p.7). In this sense the MSC cannot be seen
as simply a means of channelling and restricting responses to mass
unemployment or merely orchestrating the best efforts of the state.
It is important also to recognise its transformative role. It is
not simply absorbing or distracting the young unemployed; it is
also actively and increasingly intervening in the cultural and
material processes whereby young people learn about the nature of
wage labour, the nature of skills and of training etc. It thus
becomes a response to the political problems posed by unemployment
and by the changing nature of labour demand which simultaneously
attempts to evacuate politics from the agenda.

A TRANSFORMATIVE ATTEMPT

In this section we address two main themes: first, an identification of the central transformative work of the MSC in its interventions in 'the transition from school to work'; second, an
attempt to indicate that while the MSC's ideology and practice has
profoundly political implications, it is also vulnerable territory.
We go on to argue in our final section that it is also territory
whose contours are changing rapidly and upon which the labour movement must be active in the face of the demise of full employment,
the assault on wages, job security, craft skills and the very
quality of working life.

In the first instance, the principal transformative thrust of
the MSC has been facilitated by its ability to amplify and sustain
the myth that the major problem associated with youth unemployment

is one of a 'mismatch' between youngsters' dispositions and capacities and the characteristics required by employers. While the MSC has to acknowledge formally the critical vulnerability of its programme for the young unemployed ('Such a programme does not provide every unemployed young person with an opportunity.... Nor does it offer the guarantee of a job - *no one can do that*', MSC, 1977a, p.7, our emphasis) and concede that unemployment levels will tend to increase rather than decrease, it is nevertheless the notion of 'mismatch' which structures its provision not only for the young unemployed but also in its wider areas of involvement in education and training (e.g. in its 'Social and Life Skills' modules). Indeed, it is hard to see in what sense unemployment levels would be significantly lowered even if the 'mismatch' was eroded and a new 'correspondence' mysteriously engineered. In other words, even if the MSC was successful in imbuing the mass of the young unemployed with the necessary 'skills' and disciplines, the effect would not be to increase the number of jobs available but rather to change the nature of the competition for such jobs as may exist.

However, although the notion of 'mismatch' critically obscures the causes of unemployment and distorts the reality of 'the transition from school to work' it does promote certain political and ideological transformations. First, smothered in a rhetoric of social concern, it enables young people to be taken off the streets (and off the register) into colleges and onto courses thereby illustrating that the state is 'doing something' and 'tackling the problem'. Second, and implicitly, it locates that problem amongst the unemployed themselves. The prime focus on job finding and keeping reinforces the myth that jobs are available for those who have the 'skills', inclination and persistence to find and secure them (see chapter 9). Unemployment thus becomes a matter of individual inadequacy rather than an endemic and structural feature of a contracting labour market. Third, and as we saw in the previous chapter, it creates the political and ideological space which the great debate colonised and which invites new forms of statutory intervention in education and training and a redefinition of aims, objectives and methods. While liberal overtures are made towards equal opportunities, education for democracy, and so on, what has become clear is that the practices and policies of schooling and of post-school provision have been subordinated quite explicitly to the 'needs' of the labour market. The MSC consequently does not see itself as in any way confronting existing forms of class, sexual or racial privilege but rather is engaged in reproducing and reinforcing those fundamental distinctions which characterise a competitive system of labour market entry and endurance.

The programmes and provisions currently promoted by the MSC are not simply concerned with the transmission of 'objective' skills but rather are forms of cultural and material intervention which in this instance carry meanings about the nature of the labour market, of employment, of skills, occupational entry and wage labour and as such represent a particular example in a much more general process:

> there has never been a working class generation in this country
> that did not feel, for good or ill, the effects of state policies
> and practices which had the cumulative effect of structuring in
> certain skills, abilities, aptitudes, and so on ... and struc-

turing out (marginalising, making difficult or illegal, or ridiculous) other qualities and powers (Corrigan and Corrigan, 1977, p.3).

But this is far from a straightforward or deterministic process. These are policies, interventions and attempted transformations which are not located within a cultural and material vacuum but which are contested by alternative meanings and definitions available to the young (and, indeed, to their teachers). Consequently we would not wish crudely to denigrate the constructive and significant developments which could, for example, emerge within the new spaces opened by MSC 'Social and Life Skills' modules but rather to emphasise that such advances may only take place in the face of the constraints and ideology which underpin the nature of MSC provision (an ideology which has real, material effects in terms of funding, curricula, assessment, and so on).

As the previous chapter emphasised, it is important to recognise that the reform of education and training is in no sense a straightforward or deterministic process. Historically it has been the scene of continuing struggle and controversy. Currently the appearance of mass youth unemployment has reopened the profoundly political question of the purpose of education and training. The issues here are not simply about 'the transition from school to work' and structural unemployment but also about the nature and quality of work, about deskilling, low pay and the recomposition of labour. Institutionally the MSC is at the centre of the latest settlement and it is vital that the labour movement (and not least those trade unions most directly involved within the education and training arena) should recognise the rise of the MSC and its central role in restructuring education and training. In other words we are talking here of modes of resistance, of a continuing process of political struggle in opposition to a currently predominant ideology of education and vocational preparation which will never produce 'educated' workers (and certainly not full employment) but rather 'spare parts' for industry and the reproduction of a labour force accustomed to deskilled, intermittent employment in a labour market whose oppressive requirements go formally unquestioned.

One of the key questions here must concern the location of the MSC within this struggle. Is the Commission an accessory merely carrying out the bidding of its political masters, or is it an active accomplice in both the formulation and the distribution of the prescribed remedies? If the latter, then to whom and for what purpose? Where does the MSC stand with regard to that body of opinion which sees 'intervention' as essentially fitting workers (young or old) to the needs of the 'market' in comparison to the view that its key function should be to fit the 'market' to the needs of the workforce both employed and unemployed?

VIRTUE FROM VICE: MAGIC OR MASSAGE?

Turning to a more considered appraisal of the MSC's own particular understanding of trends apparent in the labour market we can begin to appreciate the dilemma it faces when attempting to reconcile its own views with the assumptions that inform the more powerful organs of central government.

From its early stages the MSC has developed its work around five aims:

1 to contribute to efforts to raise employment and reduce unemployment;

2 to assist manpower resources to be well developed and contribute fully to economic well being;

3 to help secure for each worker the opportunities and services he or she needs in order to lead a satisfying working life;

4 to improve the quality of decisions affecting manpower;

5 to improve the effectiveness and efficiency of the Commission.

Aims 1, 2 and 5 are noble but unremarkable for a central manpower agency. However, aims 3 and 4 do carry a hint of prescriptive activity and could, if pursued, take the MSC into some muddy political waters. After all, helping secure 'the opportunities' for workers 'to lead a satisfying working life' depends very much on a fundamental reordering of the established nature and distribution of jobs within our society if any real meaning to the term 'satisfying working life' is to be attained. And 'improving the quality of decisions affecting manpower' at a governmental level is heavily conditional upon the MSC's view of the labour market having some purchase on the process of national economic policy formulation.

This latter function is, of course, asking a lot of a relatively new agency (whose relationships with the Department of Employment and Department of Education and Science have never appeared to be particularly clear or easy) in the light of the Treasury's resolute refusal to consider anybody else's view of the economy and its policy needs but its own.

In the event, the MSC has stayed well clear of economic policy prescription. Indeed, it has gone to some lengths to protect its innocence in this regard. The 1977 'Review and Plan', in discussing the labour market, somewhat loftily remarked: 'The Commission would not wish to enter the field of overall economic policy, which would take it beyond its area of responsibility' (MSC, 1977b, para. 2.29).

Earlier, the same document had pronounced that the solution to unemployment was: 'a matter of overall economic policy which goes well beyond the competence of the commission' (ibid., para. 2.14).

One of the difficulties the Commission has faced has been the maintenance of this economic celibacy. For as the labour market has deteriorated and the MSC has been landed with growing problems to deal with it, it has required great restraint not to pass some public observations on the failures of national economic management.

In the early stages of the recession, and during the first years of the Commission, it was relatively straightforward to back governmental judgment and even adopt a fairly optimistic outlook. Both in their first and second annual reports the Commission accepted the prevailing economic wisdom that inflation and balance of payments were the prime target in so far as economic policy was concerned. The MSC role was seen in relatively simple terms as ensuring: 'that manpower bottlenecks are not allowed to develop early on in any future upturn and, in the longer run to remove structural imbalances in the labour market' (MSC, 1976a).

The Commission noted optimistically in its first annual report that unemployment had its 'positive' side in the opportunities it provided for training:

the commission suggested that a substantial increase in training activity was needed in order to prepare a stock of skills
which would have a better chance of matching the job opportunities which will open up as the economy revives (MSC, 1976a).
The authors of the second report even went so far as to observe:
'By March 1976, however, it was becoming clear that the bottom of
the recession had been reached and that the turning point for unemployment might not be delayed as long as would normally be expected' (ibid.).

By and large this style of optimism and the MSC's steady support
for the main thrust of governmental economic policy has stemmed
from a belief that unemployment was largely caused by the recession. Repeated references can be found which propound the traditional doctrine that in economic growth lies the only real path
to full employment, and that this in turn depends upon the performance of our manufacturing base: 'A regeneration of the manufacturing sector is therefore seen as the key to improving economic performance' (ibid.).

Yet alongside this equivalent of a 'stiff upper lip' approach
has been a parallel acceptance that there are major structural
factors at work which could undermine the traditional assumption
that economic growth automatically promotes employment opportunities. From the outset, the Commission noted particular difficulties
with young persons' unemployment and the disproportionate levels of
unemployment in the regions. In the case of the former it went to
great lengths in the shape of the Holland Committee to tease out
the relationship between structural and cyclical factors and the
rise in youth unemployment. However, in its 'Review and Plan'
for 1978 the MSC managed to fudge this issue with great style:

> There is some uncertainty among labour market analysts whether
> the current high level of unemployment amongst young people is
> 'structural' or 'cyclical'. In past recessions young people's
> unemployment rose more quickly than total unemployment as the
> recession set in and fell more quickly in the recovery from
> recession. It is not clear whether this pattern would still
> hold, but in the context of the Commission's planning assump-
> tions the issue does not really arise. Since unemployment seems
> likely to remain high, so too will young people's unemployment
> (MSC, 1978a).

By 1978 it was apparent that the MSC's faith in economic growth
as a provider of employment opportunities was becoming qualified.
In its report it noted that national output in the year as a whole
was 3 per cent higher than in the previous year, and that output
per person had increased by around 2.5 per cent, suggesting that
the long-term upward trend in productivity had been resumed. These
were conditions which, according to traditional assumptions, should
have produced employment growth. Indeed, employment did grow in
the 12 months to December 1978, by nearly 2000,000 - but, all of
this growth took place in the service sector (primarily in Distributive Trades, up 65,000 in 1978; Catering, 30,000; Insurance
Banking and Business Services, 30,000; Education and Medical Services about 20,000 each). In the manufacturing sector employment
declined by about 65,000 jobs, three-quarters of these being male
jobs: by contrast three-quarters of the service sector growth that
year had been in female jobs.

In the light of that evidence (which supported observations made earlier to the Commission notably by Mukherjee, 1974) that increases in output and productivity at best lead to uneven growth in employment opportunities, a subtle shift in emphasis took place. Hence the 1978 'Review and Plan' which noted a formidable 'job gap' for 1982 of 2.4 million, suggested that the 'securing of steady growth' for the economy together with the control of inflation formed: 'a necessary *precondition* for creating *some* of the jobs needed' (MSC, 1978a, para. 2.29, our emphasis).

This new-found realism has led the MSC latterly to take a far more heavily qualified view of the future. The 'Manpower Review' for 1980 (MSC, 1980b), for example, graphically compared unemployment projection to 1984 from the major forecasting organisations. These showed a growing divergence away from the government's stated assumptions. At the time the government's planning assumptions for registered unemployment were averaging 1.6 million in 1980-1 and 1.8 million in 1981-2. By comparison, the Warwick University Manpower Research Group forecast in March 1980 had registered unemployment rising from 2.1 million in 1980-1 to 2.4 million in 1981-2 (Manpower Research Group, 1980).

Although never explicitly stated, it is fairly clear that the MSC has begun to regard Treasury forecasts of unemployment as being unduly optimistic. In the 'Corporate Plan' for 1981-5, issued in April 1981 (MSC, 1981a) the Commission clearly expects unemployment to remain on a rising trend until 1983. Thereafter, forecasting becomes subject to a number of unpredictable variables, notably a change in governmental domestic policy - the authors of the Corporate Plan having implicitly recognised that this is a distinct possibility given the general election due in the following year. Nevertheless the MSC consider it prudent to: 'base our plans on unemployment staying high throughout the period up to 1985' (MSC, 1981a, para. 2.18).

Perhaps of greater significance is the comment in the following paragraph which notes: 'Even recovery starting in 1982 would have only a modest effect on unemployment during the rest of the planning period because of the long time lags involved' (ibid., para. 2.19).

How, then, has this bleaker vision of the future affected the MSC's stated aims and objectives? The latest Corporate Plan holds that the aims as laid down in 1977 (cited earlier) remain valid, but that four interlinked and equally important priority objectives can now be identified viz:

1 to safeguard the provision of skilled manpower for industry's present and future needs;
2 to ensure that all unemployed 16- and 17-year-olds have access to programmes of training and work experience, as part of efforts to improve access to training and vocational preparation for all young people;
3 to provide an efficient and cost effective employment service to meet employers' and job seekers' needs;
4 to do all that is practicable to place in permanent employment, in training or in temporary employment those unemployed job seekers who most need help in returning to work (ibid., para. 3.6).

Although this hardly indicates a total conversion to new realism,
it is clear that the MSC is no longer stressing the opportunity
for turning the vice of unemployment into the virtue of a new job
or a training opportunity.

It is important to note also that although the young unemployed
remain a high priority - the Youth Opportunities Programme is one
of the few components of the MSC programmes to have escaped expenditure cuts - they have now been joined by a concern for skill needs
and certain marginalised groups (the long-term unemployed, ethnic
minorities, disabled, etc.) as 'suitable cases for treatment'. Indeed, the MSC may now be likened more to a field ambulance struggling
to service an ever widening and ever more embattled 'front line' than
a sophisticated interventionist agency expertly planning and effect-
ing the transformation of our labour market.

In truth the expectation that the MSC would be able to wave a
magic wand over labour market 'trouble spots' has never been credible.
At best it has provided a way of massaging some of the more pressing
problems, e.g. youth unemployment, below the critical political and
public high water mark.

Latterly, however, even this ability must be open to question.
Expenditure cuts of 16 per cent in planned expenditure for 1979-80
together with 3 per cent cuts in staff levels announced towards the
end of 1979 have been boosted by further demands that the Commission
cut an extra 1,710 staff by 1984 and that £20 million be cut in
1981-2 and £30 million cut in each of the following two years. The
Commission have made the obvious point that such action can only im-
pair their performance and the service that they offer, and that at
a time when demand for assistance is at its highest.

Apart from ensuring that YOP expenditure has been increased (to
provide in excess of 400,000 places for 1981-2) the MSC's pleas appear to have fallen on deaf ears. Plainly, the present government
calculate that youth unemployment is the most sensitive political
pressure point and are therefore prepared to support MSC's efforts
in this area. However, the extent to which the government is prepared to fund their more ambitious long-term objective to provide
comprehensive training and work experience for all young people
coming on to the future labour market may well provide the acid
test. For example, such a commitment would be a good deal more expensive than existing measures for both the employed and unemployed
young (i.e. Unified Vocational Preparation (UVP) and YOP). Recent
data stemming from the MSC suggest that the gross cost in 1980
prices of providing a more comprehensive system of vocational preparation would be at least twice as much as gross expenditure on
TOP (MSC, 1981b).

Even assuming this level of expenditure was to be found acceptable, the provision of a comprehensive system of vocational preparation for 16- and 17-year-olds still begs a number of important
questions. In the first place the form and content of this new provision remains unspecified. Despite being hinted at in the Review
of the Employment and Training Act 1973 (MSC, 1980c) and more
recently touched upon in the MSC 'Corporate Plan 1981-85' (MSC,
1981a) and its 'Manpower Review' of 1981 (MSC, 1981c), detailed
proposals have yet to emerge. The consultative document due to be
published in 1981 is expected to herald, formally, the expansion of

UVP to look after the training needs of the young employed at sub-craft level. Similarly, it looks likely that the 'quality' aspect of YOP will be earmarked for expansion, e.g. Training Workshops and the better examples of Work Experience on Employers' Premises projects in order to provide a more all embracing 'traineeship' for all unemployed 16- and 17-year-olds.

However, the motivation for this remains firmly rooted in the notion that it is for the 'good' of the economy. A more comprehensive approach to vocational preparation is perceived solely in terms of improving the flexibility and adaptability of the young worker, on the assumption that, so equipped, he or she will more readily find work. Were such a policy to be directly linked to policies on early retirement, some immediate benefits might accrue. As it stands, however, improving vocational preparation for the young, whilst eminently desirable, is only a partial answer for the workforce as a whole. Unless equal attention is given to other methods of reducing labour supply such as reduced working time, adult retraining and early retirement then improving the 'employ-ability' of young workers may do little more than transfer unemployment further along the age range.

Fitting the worker to the market can only be valid if the market is going to return to some sort of growth in labour demand. In this sense an Easter Promise is apposite in that the work-force involved will remain firmly nailed to the 'Cross' which this orthodox assumption has erected. The resurrection will have to wait until the policy makers switch their attention to fitting the 'market' to the work-force.

NOTES

1 This analysis draws heavily on the work of Dan Finn and Simon Frith (1980).

Chapter 6

TRADES UNIONS AND SPECIAL MEASURES FOR THE YOUNG UNEMPLOYED

Denis Gregory and Christine Noble

INTRODUCTION

During the post-war period successive governments, with the exception of the present administration, have accepted an increasingly
interventionist role in order to guide the performance of the economy and to shape our industrial structure. Whilst this reflects
the influence of Keynesian economics and a political commitment to
the maintenance of full employment, it has equally been seen as a
necessary response to the fundamental changes which have taken
place in world trading patterns, together with other factors which
have threatened the UK's economic stability and growth.

The response of the trade-union movement has been critically
dependent upon the intentions and consequences which have been
ascribed to interventionist policies. This inevitably led to closer
relationships and harmony with the labour governments headed by Wil-
son and Callaghan in the 1960s and 1970s.

These latter administrations saw the development of much greater
involvement by the Trades Union Congress (TUC) in the formation and
implementation of economic policy. For example, a tripartite structure was adopted to embrace the industrial 'partners': the TUC and
the Confederation of British Industry (CBI) together with government representatives, at both the National Economic Development
Organisation (NEDO) and the Manpower Services Commission (MSC). The
former was responsible for the last labour government's industrial
strategy (developed by tripartite sector working parties) whilst
the latter, as we shall see, was responsible for implementing government policy in the labour market.

The trade-union response to the special measures implemented by
the MSC has to be seen against this backcloth in a functional sense,
but equally the importance of the political and overtly bipartite
'social contract' concluded between the trade-union movement and
the Callaghan administration should not be ignored. It was through
this understanding that the TUC was able to pressurise the government 'to do something' about the growing problem of youth unemployment.

In addition, the spirit of the'social contract', together with
the commitment to tripartitism ensured (seemingly) positive trade-

union involvement in the approval and running of the special measures. The action committees, which had been lashed together to
oversee the Job Creation Programme (JCP), gave way to a more
sophisticated network of 28 Area Boards set up at local level to
help administer the Youth Opportunities Programme (YOP) and the
Special Temporary Employment Programme (STEP).

On the face of it, this combination of a political consensus
uniting the union movement with the government on the need to 'do
something' about youth unemployment and a structure at local level
set to involve and utilise trade-union representatives would appear
to offer a strong platform on which interventions into the youth
labour market could be based. In general terms this indeed proved
to be the case - the political unity overcoming early fears concerning JCP and the Work Experience Programme (WEP), whilst the
involvement of the TUC in the Holland Committee brought sufficient
credibility to launch YOP and see it through its first year of operation without any major trade-union challenges.

However, the platform on which the special measures were launched
has become increasingly unsteady. It is not the fault of either the
MSC or YOP that the 'social contract' was first ruptured and then
finally killed off when the government changed in 1979. Similarly,
neither the MSC nor any of the special measures can be blamed for
the continuing rise in the general level of unemployment with its
attendant adverse effects on the long-term and 'prime age' unemployed.
Clearly, both of these factors have played a part in calling into
question the broad trade-union support that was given to YOP and
STEP. However, there are further important factors which have contributed to trade-union doubts over which the MSC has had some control.

For example, the MSC must shoulder some of the responsibility for
failing to ensure that the Area Board structure could operate effective controls at local level over the approval and monitoring of
individual schemes. It is also clear that the MSC has failed,
despite a concerted effort, to improve significantly the quality
of individual schemes. Faced with a rapidly deteriorating youth
labour market and the need to expand the places available on YOP
with equal speed, one can see the dilemma in which the MSC has
found itself. None the less, an appreciation of the logistic problem merely begs the equally important questions concerning the fit-
ness and the purpose of the special measures. It is these latter
questions which, in the last year or so, have come to the fore-
front in so far as many trade unionists are concerned.

The rest of this chapter will attempt to trace some of the key
elements which have underpinned and fashioned the trade-union
approach to the young unemployed. The implications of the current
debate on the importance of structural as opposed to cyclical factors in the causation of youth unemployment are sketched whilst the
legitimacy of trade-union criticisms of the special measures (primarily YOP) are examined in the light of recent work carried out in
Wales and the North West of England.

Before moving on to these issues, however, it is worthwhile
briefly sketching the development of the TUC's thinking on youth
unemployment.

THE ORTHODOX VIEW

The established trade-union view of young people in the labour market has emphasised consistently the need for more attention to be
paid by government and employers alike to job related training and
education for young workers. From the 'Youth Charter' accepted at
the Annual Congress of 1938, the continued emphasis of the TUC has
been focused on these areas. It was highly significant that the
immediate response of the TUC to the first major post-war problem
of youth unemployment, i.e. that arising in 1971, was to reiterate
demands for improved day-release and training facilities for all
16- to 18-year-olds to give them better employment chances. In 1972
the General Council had made a clear linkage between lack of training, the needs of modern industry and subsequent employment opportunities for young people:

> In the General Council's view all young workers should receive
> some training relating to their employment since it is increas-
> ingly clear that in the absence of training an increasing num-
> ber of young workers will be virtually unemployable in modern
> industry (TUC, 1972, p.417).

It should be recognised that prior to 1971, trade-union judgments
on the needs of young people in or out of work had been formed
against the backcloth of 25 years of virtually full employment for
school-leavers and young people. The problems perceived were not
so much as getting a job but rather were related to the terms and
conditions attached to the job - hence the emphasis on improving
training and educational facilities.

The advent of a persistently high level of youth unemployment
(masked for a couple of years, following the raising of the school-
leaving age) has not shifted the TUC from its orthodoxy. For example, Hugh Scanlon, in a motion to Congress in 1976, called for an
expansion of 'apprenticeships and other training opportunities'
together with 'the provision of more full time and day release educational courses for 16 to 18 year olds.' Moreover, Len Murray, in
a first attempt to bring YOP to the attention of the wider trade-
union movement, made it clear that he endorsed the programme partly
because 'some lessons which will be of long term value' would be
available if, in the MSC programme, 'some new forms of vocational
preparation are piloted' (TUC, 1978). However, the deteriorating
labour market for young people has brought with it a need for additional responses to complement the established line. In the short
to medium term, the practical response has been to endorse officially the development of the special measures and commend them to
trade unionists as a reasonable, if only temporary, approach towards
the solution of youth unemployment. Indeed, in 'A Chance Would be a
Fine Thing' the TUC takes the credit for proposing the Work Experience Programme to the government (TUC, 1978a, p.11). More recently
the TUC's document 'Unemployment, The Fight for TUC Alternatives'
calls for a further expansion of YOP and for more cash to be channelled into apprenticeships (TUC, 1981a, p.20).

The longer term, more permanent solutions tend to emerge when
the present recession or structural factors are considered to be
at the root of high levels of youth unemployment. The structural
factors explanation holds that a major change in the demand for

labour within a particular industry or sector which has not been caused by short run fluctuations in the trade cycle is leading to job displacement. Hence, job losses arising from the application of new technology or even simply the introduction of new working methods are regarded as having structural causes. Similarly, shifts in employer preferences, say towards married women return- ing to the work-force and away from unemployed, inexperienced school-leavers gives rise to what has been termed a 'structural' mismatch, where the new job opportunities being created do not match the attributes of the pool of unemployed labour available.

Even when the TUC has considered unemployment a longer term problem, however, in terms of its suggestions for a solution, ortho- doxy still appears to be ascendant. It is clear from the 1981 TUC Economic Review (TUC, 1981b) that reflation of the economy on a relatively standard Keynesian model, e.g. by pumping £6 billion into public expenditure, is seen as the only permanent means of securing and creating employment. Some recognition of structural factors is afforded by the acknowledgment given to the importance of reducing working time. However, there is little visible support for the direct linking of measures to reduce working time with the creation of employment opportunities specifically for young people.

It is this emphasis on policies designed to cope with a reces- sion which has tended to validate what has been, in effect, a some- what dismissive approach adopted by the TUC and individual trade unions towards the MSC's special measures. At best they have been regarded as a temporary palliative, a stopgap until the real battle to get the economy 'on the move again' - and some real jobs created - is won.

This is not to say that the TUC's analysis and related policy is without foundation. There is certainly ample statistical evidence (most notably from Makeham's study (1980)) to show the strong corre- lation between the increase in the general level of unemployment and that of young people in particular. Similarly, during the up- turn in previous post-war trade cycles, the labour market for young people has tended to recover faster than for the unemployed as a whole. The question remains, however, what if the rise and current level of youth unemployment owes more to structural rather than re- cessional factors?

There are ominous signs to suggest that this may be the case. The Holland report highlighted the demographic changes leading to steadily increasing numbers of school-leavers entering the labour market between 1976-81. This general pressure on opportunities for young people is further accentuated for girls by the increas- ing participation of married women 'returning' to the labour mar- ket and competing with school-leavers and young women for available jobs (since the difference in wage costs between these groups is relatively small, the greater stability offered by married women is tending to give them the edge in a tight labour market).

Moreover, throughout the post-war period, irrespective of boom or slump, the economy has undergone a structural occupational change which has seen employment in manufacturing decline with a particu- larly marked fall in male jobs. Employment in the service sector has by contrast grown. The decline in employment in manufacturing has been underpinned by the fall in the UK share of world trade in manufactured goods (from 20 per cent in 1950 down to around 8 per cent currently), but it probably owes far more to the substitution of capital for labour, i.e. the use of machines rather than man- power in its drive for profitability. Even with unprecedented economic growth it is unlikely that this well-established trend will reverse - indeed the advent of the micro-processor is more likely to result in the accelerated decline of jobs in the manu- facturing sector.

The growth in the service sector has depended crucially upon a parallel growth in government expenditure on public services. Since 1976 this expenditure growth has been progressively restrained to the point where, under the present administration, actual expendi- ture has fallen (in real terms) substantially in key sectors, e.g. housing and construction. Even assuming a return to public expen- diture growth we cannot be assured that employment opportunities will similarly respond since the effects of new technology on the service sector may well exert a strong counterbalancing influence. Be that as it may, and even allowing for a neutral impact, it will make little difference on the demand for young people. Recent evidence shows that first-time entrants into the labour market were concentrated precisely in those sectors suffering from the worst structural changes (Department of Employment, 1980). For example, in 1978, 16-year-old boys were less likely to be found in the service industries than was true for males as a whole but more likely to be found in construction, whereas girls were less likely to be employed in the service industries relative to total female employment but more likely to be found in manufacturing.

Moreover, we should not disregard the fact that as unemployment has climbed (officially) to over 3 million, an increasing number of skilled, prime age workers have been thrown out of work. In the event of an upturn in the economy, a combination of societal fac- tors, which will include strong trade-union pressure and economic forces, will, in all probability, force these individuals to the head of the queue for newly created jobs. The speed with which an upturn in economic activity translates into job opportunities for young workers will then depend upon the length of time it takes to reallocate this stratum of prime age and skilled workers to the employed labour force.

If this alternative view of the underlying causes of youth un- employment proves valid, then the trade-union movement may well have to come to terms with the need for a more or less permanent version of a form of Youth Opportunities Programme. It is appro- priate then to turn our attention to a more detailed analysis of how trade unions have reacted to the type of interventions which have taken place in the youth labour market.

EXPERIENCE OR EXPLOITATION?

Some background

The Job Creation Programme was the first attempt at intervention in the labour market agreed by the government in 1973 and handed to the MSC to implement. It was this hastily planned exercise which

subsequently fashioned the basis of the trade union response to
the special measures which followed. For example, the common term
used by trade unionists to describe the special measures remains
'Job Creation'. The implication of this imprint will be considered
more fully in later paragraphs. At this stage it is sufficient
merely to note that whilst the first contact with short run interventions of this kind did not staunch the flow of trade-union demands for more to be done for the young unemployed, it nevertheless
raised a number of questions and provoked fears amongst active
trade unionists that have never satisfactorily been removed by the
experience of the later special measures.

Doing 'more for the young unemployed' translated into the launch
of WEP in 1976. Aimed specifically at providing a period of work
experience at the workplace for the unemployed school-leaver and
17-year-old, this programme potentially impinged far more onto traditional trade-union territory due to the fact that it paid a non-
negotiated rate fixed well below either junior or apprentice rates
applicable in the generality of the labour market. Moreover, the
notion that young people could gain useful work experience in a
supernumerary capacity without at some stage or other either duplicating or replacing the effort of ordinary full-time workers was
never an easy idea for shop stewards to accept. In fact this idea
owes far more to the naivety of the Civil Service architects of
WEP than to the experience of the average shop-steward. This early
example of the gap between normative prescription and actual practice provided a powerful factor undermining the credibility of MSC
schemes with trade-union activists at workplace level. Again, WEP
triggered certain critical responses which have persisted through
the development of YOP and have latterly (1981) caused certain
major unions to speak out strongly against the way in which the
Work Experience on Employers Premises (WEEP) component of YOP has
been operated.

All this has left the TUC in a difficult and ambiguous position.
On the one hand, the General Council were strong proponents of the
Holland committee, and representatives from the TUC both served on
the committee and signed the subsequent report. In turn, the recommendation of Holland (in effect the establishment of YOP and STEP)
were endorsed at the TUC Annual Congress thus conferring the TUC
'seal of approval'. On the other hand, some three years on, a few
major affiliated unions are now arguing that the practice of YOP is
constituting a major threat to their membership and that union support for the programme should be withdrawn.

SPECIFIC CRITICISMS: 'COSMETIC', DIVERSIONARY', 'EXPLOITATION'

Trade-union criticism of the MSC's interventionist measures tend to
fall into three broad categories. First of all the measures have
been frequently described as being purely cosmetic, that is, that
they were a device for reducing the level of registered unemployed
in order to lower the political 'heat' generated by high levels of
youth unemployment. Furthermore, the schemes were seen to be an
emergency response (JCP was in fact so described by the Secretary
of State for Employment on its introduction), temporary in nature

and therefore incapable of providing a real solution to the creation of additional permanent job opportunities for young people.

Second, the measures were seen to be diversionary in that it
was (and is) felt that the money voted for short-term job creation
and work-experience purposes would have been (and could be) better
used to create either additional full-time apprenticeships, or permanent jobs by boosting public expenditure in certain sectors,
e.g. housing and construction.

Third, it is strongly argued that the young unemployed and ordinary employed workers alike are exploited by the operation, particularly WEEP.   The principal fears at work here are that the
young worker taken into this part of YOP will be utilised as cheap
labour and, in addition, that he or she will not receive a proper
training or work experience.   Either way the youngster could be
exploited and the employment security of other workers consequently
threatened.

It is this latter fear which has recently translated into strong
criticisms of the programme from the National Union of Public Employees (NUPE) and the Union of Shop Distributive and Allied Workers
(USDAW) in particular. Against a backcloth of sharply rising unemployment it was perhaps inevitable that this type of backlash
against YOP should take place, but how valid are these trade-union
criticisms?

Certainly it cannot be denied that the measures are and have been
'cosmetic' (although the label might be disputed) in that they have
not created additional jobs for young people. However, in fairness
no such claims were ever made for the schemes. What has been said
in their defence is that the experience offered to the young unemployed has improved their subsequent chances of finding permanent
employment. At the start of YOP a placement rate of 80 per cent
was reported. More recently, however, the placement rate has
dropped - the last publicly quoted figure put it at around 36 per
cent. Unconfirmed reports from trade unionists involved in running
various schemes have put it as low as 10 per cent. Whilst the placement rate into permanent employment remained high, trade-union criticisms of the 'cosmetic' nature of the schemes had little influence
on trade-union support. However, with a falling placement rate a
more potent criticism has emerged to the effect that YOP raises
expectations which it cannot fulfill, the inference being that this
is only marginally less damaging to a young person than is the experience of uninterrupted unemployment. It is difficult to judge
whether this is in fact the case (there appears to be no systematic
research findings available to confirm or refute the suggestion),
but the credibility of YOP will be materially impaired if it can be
demonstrated that time spent on the programme is making no difference to the employment chances of the youngsters involved.

A charge less easy to substantiate is that the special programmes
have been diversionary in so far as financial resources are concerned.
The amount of money devoted to special programmes theoretically
could have been spent elsewhere in the public sector to create permanent employment, for example, in housing. In practice, given that
both the present and previous government were committed to expenditure restraint, there could be no guarantee that money saved on YOP
would in fact be spent in this way. However, with regard to the

internal allocation of resources at the MSC, the position is somewhat different.

In the first place, although expenditure on YOP has been one of
the few elements of the MSC's budget to emerge unscathed, there is
to date little to suggest that other parts of the MSC's operations
have been cut back in order solely to release resources for YOP.
Rather it would seem that the rest of the MSC's activities have
simply fallen foul of the government's expenditure cutting crusade.
Moreover, in spite of this the MSC still managed to provide extra
expenditure to bolster the reduction in apprenticeships offered in
industry in general in 1980.

However, in the four years to 1984-5, special employment measures
will significantly cut into the MSC's overall budgetary allocation.
Between 1976-7 and 1980-1 these special measures accounted for
around £760 million out of total MSC expenditure of £3,506 million –
about 22 per cent. By comparison between 1981-2 and 1984-5 expenditure on special measures is projected to increase to £1,578 million
out of a total of £3,375 million. In other words special measures
will account for nearly half (46.8 per cent) of the commission's
total expenditure over the four year period.

During the growth of expenditure on special employment measures
(JCP, WEP, YOP and STEP) over the period 1976 to 1980-1, the balance
of provision for other MSC activities, principally the Employment
Services Division (ESD) and the Training Services Division (TSD) has
remained fairly stable but in the next four years this is set to
decline significantly. In the case of TSD, there is to be a cut in
the Training Opportunities courses (TOPS) and a reduction in direct
training services; also expenditure on services to industrial training boards in 1984-5 will be 25 per cent down on that of 1980-1. ESD
is less affected but will still have to cut expenditure by 10 per
cent mainly through economies at job centres and local employment
offices.

Thus, over the next four years MSC resources will be reduced in
order to make way for increased spending on YOP and the Community
Employment Project (CEP). This must cast considerable doubt over
the ability of the MSC to undertake any development of training
programmes which are not specifically catered for by the proposed
expansion of YOP and CEP. Given the high level of general unemployment expected to prevail over the next three years or so, one
is forced to conclude that this may prove an unhealthily narrow
concentration of the MSC's efforts. It remains to be seen whether
trade unions see this reallocation of resources within the budget
as prudent or diversionary.

Fears that individual schemes are being 'abused' by unscrupulous
employers have emerged as the most potent trade-union criticism of
YOP. Under the general banner of 'exploitation', a number of individual worries can be discerned, in no particular order they appear
as follows:

(a) that because young persons taken on under YOP are paid a
fixed allowance by the MSC which is set some way below the negotiated rates for young full-time employees and apprentices, they
represent a supply of cheap labour to an individual employer;
(b) arising from this, any employer utilising YOP trainees to
fill gaps in his/her regular work-force sets up a substitution

effect at the workplace to the detriment of ordinary full time
workers;

(c) that employers use the YOP period to 'try out' young workers, thereby subverting their normal recruitment practices.
This six months 'free' trial period could be used to evaluate
young workers for full-time job vacancies which may have existed
when one YOP period started and should have been filled straight
away;

(d) that youngsters on YOP are merely used as an 'extra pair of
hands' and therefore secure no systematic training or properly
structured programme of work experience;

(e) that youngsters have their expectations of a full-time job
raised by their experience on YOP only to have them cruelly
dashed by a return to the dole queue at the end of the YOP
period ('there is no guarantee of a job at the end – they are
just thrown back on the scrap heap').

Although here referred to in the context of YOP, most of these
fears originated amongst trade unionists who observed the operation
of JCP and more particularly WEEP. Moreover, unless one believes
that individual employers are highly charged with altruistic motives
towards the young, it can be seen that the concerns raised above
are by no means merely truculent gripings from organisations whose
priorities preclude the needs of the young unemployed.

Accordingly, between 1978 and 1980, the Trade Union Research
Unit at Ruskin College, Oxford, together with the William Temple
Foundation in Manchester set out to evaluate the extent to which
these fears were borne out by the experience of YOP. Two surveys
of shop stewards were carried out to sound trade-union opinion of
the special measures and youth unemployment in general, utilising
the networks of the Wales TUC and the North West Regional Council
of the TUC. In addition, case studies were carried out of unionised
workplaces that had or were participating in YOP. Interviews with
trade-union members of MSC area boards in the two regions were also
undertaken to monitor the development of trade union involvement
at this particular level (see Gregory et al., 1979; Gregory and
Edgar, 1980).

The shop-stewards survey, albeit carried out with different
populations in 1978 and 1980, allowed a comparison of trade-union
attitudes during the first two years of YOP. In the first place,
some general opinions clearly did not change over the time period:

(a) that school-leavers as a specific group were the hardest hit
by the increase in unemployment;

(b) that the persistently high level of unemployment was largely
caused by deficient demand management and therefore required
traditional reflationary measures as a solution rather than short-
term interventions;

(c) that the special measures for young people were 'better than
nothing' but they were too short and since there was no guarantee
of a permanent job at the end were inadequate as anything more
than an emergency response;

(d) that the fixed allowance paid was too low and should in any
event have been subject to local negotiations to ensure a proper
rate.

Over the period the shop-stewards' level of knowledge of YOP did increase, but not perhaps as fast as the MSC would have liked: for example, in both 1978 and 1980 about one-third of our respondents reported no knowledge at all of YOP. Perhaps the most significant change, however, lay in the perception of which particular section of the unemployed deserved special action in order to improve their chances of securing full-time employment. Although an invidious question in many ways (as many of the respondents pointed out), in the early survey school-leavers were clearly singled out as the section of the unemployed most deserving of special attention. By 1980 this preference was by no means as clear cut. Although school-leavers remained a high priority, they tended to be joined by 'family men' as requiring special attention. This shift was almost entirely related to both the spread of long-term unemployment into the 'prime age' work-force and a pessimistic outlook on future employment trends.

This is not to say that experience of YOP has allayed the classic fears of exploitation listed earlier. Although neither survey revealed strong evidence of actual exploitation (for example, in 1980 only 15 per cent of the respondents felt that exploitation was a disadvantage with WEEP), there were clear indications that the potential for abuse was strongly suspected. Hence great stress was laid on establishing job security safeguards for the full-time work-force as important pre-conditions to the acceptance of YOP at any particular workplace.

Fears of exploitation were also strongly differentiated according to whether the respondent had had specific contact with YOP or its predecessors. Experience tended to allay the fears. Our case studies showed that where a proper course of consultation had been undertaken, followed by a visible involvement of local trade unionists in the running of schemes, widespread support was readily mobilised for the continuation of the programme. A shop-steward from a major plant in Wales illustrated the point: 'As the shop floor people saw this the comments we were getting were that we should have had the scheme years ago' (Shop-steward, BSC Trostre). Despite such evidence of support, trade-union suspicion, particularly of WEEP, has continued to grow. In part this has arisen as a result of a failure to locate WEEP in trade-union organised workplaces. Although precise data are hard to come by, the MSC admit that WEEP placements are predominantly located in small workplaces. It is possible that as many as 75 per cent of WEEP youngsters lie outside of the formal organised networks of the trade-union movement. In this sense some of the trade-union fears of 'abuse' are based on secondhand information. Nevertheless, the distrust of the small employer (whether justified or not) is a potent force within the trade-union movement, whilst the MSC's current concern with substitution and the reports of its own surveys which suggest that it may be taking place in some 30 per cent of schemes has tended to validate what may otherwise have been passed off as a traditionally sceptical view.

The totality of trade-union criticism of YOP can perhaps best be understood as a fusing of a static set of fears with a dynamic understanding of what is happening in the labour market. Thus, concern over exploitation arises rather more from the perceived weakness of

the programme, in that it is felt to be inherently open to abuse -
paying a low non-negotiated allowance, with no job security and
little by way of official provision for monitoring - rather than as
a result of direct experience. Conversely, fears with regard to
substitution (leaving aside the MSC's own evidence) are increasingly
informed by the reality of a collapsing labour market, such that
those unions who have had extensive contact with YOP, for example
NUPE in the public services and local authority sector and USDAW in
distribution, have been forced into ever more defensive positions.
One example of this has recently been provided by NUPE in Wales who
threatened publicly to withdraw support from YOP in the Principality.
The reasons given were the inadequacy of the fixed allowance paid
to YOP trainees, the failure of the prior consultation and approval
procedures at local level and the overall fear that YOP was being
used to plug the manpower gaps which had resulted from expenditure
cutbacks. The threat was suspended subject to a reference to the
TUC for an urgent meeting with both the MSC and the Secretary of
State over the need to raise the allowance, together with the drawing up and issuing of new guidelines to tighten up the procedures
whereby union approval is sought for a particular scheme.

The dilemma for MSC and TUC alike, particularly accentuated in
the public sector where YOP has been extensively applied, is that
at a time when an increasing number of YOP places need to be found
(to meet the anticipated increase in youth unemployment in 1981-2),
major unions are less willing to accept 'temporary' youngsters in
workplaces when their adult members are being put outside 'on the
cobbles' in increasing numbers. Thus, even if improvements are
gained with respect to both the allowance paid to YOP trainees and
the procedures for consulting and winning the consent of unions
locally, the problems of a collapsed labour market, i.e. increased
prime age unemployment and a greater incidence of long term unemployment, will continue to harden union attitudes to YOP.

What then of the future? Are there any changes in prospect
which could affect a reversal of what appears to be an increasingly
critical union view of YOP?

In the short run some changes do appear feasible and would make
a helpful contribution. Important here is an urgent need to initiate a prior consultation and approval mechanism. Merely request-
ing that a sponsor indicates on the YOP application form whether
union approval is (a) necessary and (b) has been gained is wholly
inadequate and is in fact less informative than the questions con-
tained on the early JCP forms. Unions are particularly sensitive
about adequate prior consultation before a scheme is implemented.
Hence, some minimum time period should be specified for consultation.
In addition, the level at which approval is sought and the means by
which the process is carried out is also in need of clarification.
A telephone conversation to a busy full-time official may be con-
venient but it is not sufficient and was shown by our case studies
to be counterproductive: it sometimes caused resentment amongst the
union's lay representatives who were affected by the particular
scheme. By comparison, the submitting to the appropriate trade-
union branch officials of the details of a proposed scheme prior to
submission to the MSC may prove more cumbersome and long winded,
but as one case study of a major local authority in North Wales

showed, is also the only effective means of securing meaningful trade-union co-operation.

Union confidence in the MSC's ability to 'weed out' the more contentious YOP proposals would similarly be enhanced if the rules governing the operation of the twenty-eight area boards were changed. From their inception these bodies have only reviewed those individual proposals which offered more than twenty places. This rule, doubt-less originally framed with an eye to administrative expediency, has effectively removed from the scrutiny of the area board members the majority of WEEP proposals, and certainly has pre-empted the more dubious ones (e.g. from the corner shop, massage parlour or turf accountants), in so far as the trade unions are concerned, from being properly vetted. This has led many unionists to conclude that the boards are merely 'rubber stamping operations': a situa-tion made no easier by the fact that for many trade-union activists the existing MSC-organised District Manpower Committees (DMCs) al-ready offered a proven network, tripartite in composition and with a better purchase on local labour market information. Improvements to the present position would seem, then, to lie between opening up access to all YOP proposals for individual board members and the abandonment of the area boards in favour of the DMCs. A more sen-sible compromise might be to devolve some part of the vetting of proposals to the DMC, for example those involving small-scale em-ployers who fell within the geographical area covered by the DMC.

Further short-run improvements could be gained in terms of the fixing of the weekly allowance and the provision of off-the-job education for YOP trainees. While the weekly allowance remains some way below the negotiated junior rates for industry and com-merce, unions will always be uneasy. Moreover, the fact that they have seemingly played no part in reaching the figure merely com-pounds the felony: 'I personally believe that it is a ridiculous wage, I wonder who on earth negotiated it in the first place' (T&GWU Branch Secretary in Wales on the YOP allowance). It is not surprising, therefore, that individual unions like NUPE and the Transport and General Workers' Union (T&GWU) are currently pressur-ising for the allowance to be increased. Although this is inevit-ably bound up with the threat which 'cheap labour' imposes, there was also plentiful evidence from our two shop-steward surveys that there was a general feeling that youngsters employed on the special measures (with the exception of JCP which paid the going rate) were hard done by as far as remuneration was concerned.

Irrespective of what final figure is eventually reached, the present position would definitely be improved if a trade-union body was to be recognised for the purpose of bargaining the allowance annually with the MSC.

For some time, the TUC has advocated the improvement and increase of off-the-job training provision for YOP participants. This is seen as being desirable in itself, but also as a counter to the possibilities of using YOP trainees as mere substitutes for full-time workers. In fairness, the MSC has made strong efforts to im-prove this aspect of YOP, raising participation in off-the-job training from around 10 per cent of all trainees to around 33 per cent currently. The fact that two out of every three YOP youngsters do not enjoy the benefits of a day or half a day away from the workplace is, however, a measure of the improvement that could be made.

In the medium term, all or most of these criticisms may be over-come by the implementation of the MSC's eagerly awaited new train-ing initiative. At the time of writing little detail has emerged, but it would appear that one of the major union criticisms of YOP - that it is a temporary measure - has been recognised: the new initiative has been widely foreshadowed (see MSC 1981a; 1981c) as offering a permanent commitment to providing a comprehensive pro-gramme of vocational preparation for all young people (whether in or out of employment) up to the age of 18. The extent to which the new initiative will meet with union approval remains to be seen. Certainly if it is to succeed it will need to build on the advan-tages of its permanency and meet the other criticisms outlined in this chapter. Moreover, if, in the meantime, YOP is to continue to enjoy trade-union support and co-operation, it will need to be seen as an essential part of the transition to this permanent pro-vision of a foundation of training and work experience open to all young people. Even then, the dramatic collapse of the labour mar-ket visible in the last twelve months must render any major exten-sion of YOP problematic.

Finally, the trade-union criticisms of YOP described here should not be seen, as is suggested in some quarters, as reflecting a parochial view of 'defending the members' interests'. The fact that the unemployed young are not in trade-union membership has made no difference to the pressure which the TUC has imposed on the MSC and successive governments for action on their behalf. It is more accurate to say that unions see the basic needs of the young unemployed as being identical to those of any unemployed per-son. Trade-union concern may appear to be shifting towards the prime-age worker and the long-term unemployed. In reality, this represents a spreading not a worsening of trade-union concern. However, it means that support for an interventionist policy which is geared to a specific age group must be actively worked for rather than merely taken for granted.

NOTES

1 This chapter is partly based upon research projects funded by the European Commission and the Manpower Services Commission, whose support is gratefully acknowledged.

Chapter 7

THE JOB CREATION PROGRAMME: SOME REFLECTIONS ON ITS PASSING

Graham Markall

> Now, all these measures, the extension of the temporary employ-
> ment subsidy, the work creation scheme and the recruitment
> subsidy for school leavers, will start before the end of this
> year - some of them I hope in the next week or two - and will
> come to an end by the end of next year (Denis Healey, 'Financial
> Times', 25 September 1975).

Denis Healey's prediction was at least partly true. Within three
weeks of his announcement the Manpower Services Commission (MSC)
had introduced its Job Creation Programme (JCP) and thus 'the work
creation scheme' was launched 'to alleviate the worst effects of
the highest level of unemployment since the war' (MSC, 1976a, p.2).
As the chancellor implied, the new programme was seen as essentially a 'counter cyclical measure' (MSC, 1976b, p.18) and to represent nothing more than 'contingency plans' (MSC, 1976a, p.4) in
anticipation of an economic revival. But the deepening recession
confounded even mildly optimistic assumptions about the economy
and in the spring of 1977, some months after the original temporary measures were supposed to have disappeared, the MSC published
its observations on 'Young People and Work' (The Holland Report)
and was forced to remark: 'Even on optimistic assumptions about
the British economy, the success of the Industrial Strategy and
the creation of new jobs, the numbers of young people out of work
will remain historically high at least until 1981' (MSC, 1977a,
p.7).

The severity of the problem was recognised and high levels of
youth unemployment acknowledged to be at least a medium-term feature
of the economy if not a structural one. The response was 'that an
essentially ad hoc approach should be replaced by a new programme
of opportunities for young people' (MSC, 1977a, p.7) and the original emergency responses, JCP included, were reorganised and massively
expanded to become the Youth Opportunities Programme (YOP) which
emerged in the Spring of 1978. Nevertheless, JCP survived until
the end of that same year (some two years longer than Denis Healey's
original decree) whilst undergoing its assimilation into the new
YOP development and in acknowledging its passing the MSC paid tri-
bute to its contribution:

Very many young people have been given opportunities which they would never otherwise have had. These opportunities have been of a new kind which have attracted and engaged young people and shown that they can help in a practical way those who have achieved little or nothing at school or in more traditional forms of provision. There can be little doubt that the schemes mounted so far have added significantly to the general stock of skills in this country (MSC, 1977a, p,29).

It is the aim of this paper to examine the 'new kind' of 'opportunities' offered by JCP, to assess the nature of the 'general stock of skills' supposedly promoted by its existence and to identify in what way it helped 'those who have achieved little or nothing at school or in more traditional forms of provision.' It attempts to do so by offering a case study of one particular JCP scheme – the Oldfield Painting and Decorating Project (OPDP) – as it operated in an inner-city area in the north west of England.

By way of explanation there is a brief account of its operation but the prime focus here is not upon a detailed description of its historical development but upon the formal goals of JCP in general and the outcome of the OPDP's attempt in particular to achieve them. Obviously, as with any case study, evidence can only be illustrative rather than definitive but by using particular evidence and with reference to specific elements and characteristics of the OPDP, an attempt will be made to explore two broad themes. First, to examine critically some key features of the JCP initiative through a study of this one scheme's implementation of MSC guidelines and to assess the consequences of their translation into practice. Second, to attempt to identify the ruptures and shifts, as well as the continuities, which informed the transition from JCP to YOP and to gauge their impact upon youngsters such as those with whom the OPDP dealt and whose interests the MSC claims to be promoting.

THE OPDP: A BRIEF ACCOUNT OF ITS OPERATION

The OPDP sprang from an early response to the introduction of JCP taken by a voluntary organisation based in a city in the north west of England. Following MSC guidelines, the organisation drew up and submitted proposals for a painting and decorating project to operate in an inner-city area, which shall be called Oldfield, adjacent to the city's docks. The proposals were accepted by MSC and in May 1976 the OPDP was established. It was testimony both to the growing permanence of the 'special measures' and to the status of the OPDP that its original allotted lifespan of only six months was extended repeatedly until it ultimately ran the full term of JCP's own duration until the end of 1978.

The work of the OPDP centred upon the redecoration of homes in the Oldfield neighbourhood. Because JCP projects were not allowed to impinge upon established commercial operations, the OPDP had to undertake that its work would be solely with householders who would not otherwise be able to redecorate their homes in the normal course of events and through the normal commercial channels. Consequently clients were only to be drawn from the ranks of those who were deemed to be suitably impoverished.

Potential clients qualified according to any one of three
criteria:

1 If they were claiming supplementary benefit from the local
office of the Department of Health and Social Security (DHSS)
and agreed to pay the OPDP for the cost of materials used in
redecorating. Labour costs were met by JCP in the normal way.
(This group represented approximately 25 per cent of all
clients.)

2 If they were claiming supplementary benefit and the local
office of the DHSS agreed to pay for the cost of materials
used in redecorating on the basis of an 'exceptional needs
payment'.

3 If they were not claiming supplementary benefit but nevertheless the local office of the DHSS agreed to administer an
'exceptional needs payment' for the purposes of redecoration.
(These last two groups represented approximately 75 per cent
of all clients.)

There were usually around twenty-two workers on the OPDP work-
force consisting of one project co-ordinator, one administrative
assistant, two supervisors and a fluctuating number of young
workers. With the exception of one female administrative assistant the entire work-force was male.

The project co-ordinator was with the OPDP throughout its lifetime and his task was not only to regulate the OPDP work-force
according to JCP criteria and to resolve the usual difficulties
concerning insurance, tax problems and the payment of wages etc.,
but also it was through him that the work of the project was con-
trolled and directed.

The supervisors worked very closely with the project co-ordinator
in costing jobs and informing him when they expected one to be completed so that he in turn could inform the next client when work
would start in his or her home. They also provided constant information on the flow of materials, warned of shortages and ensured that materials were always in supply. In addition they were
responsible for reporting any difficulties with employees to the
co-ordinator (e.g. in terms of absenteeism, misbehaviour, etc.) and
also provided guidance for the young workers by illustrating decorating techniques and explaining how to tackle different problems. This
was by no means a formal or intensive process but was performed very
much in an ad hoc manner before a job was started. Thereafter the
youngsters were left very much to their own devices, operating in
teams of two, although there was usually a brief daily visit from
a supervisor to check on the progress of the job and to ensure that
there was no shortage of materials. When a particular job was completed the supervisor would transfer all the necessary equipment to
the next location.

In terms of its workload, the project's contacts came from a
variety of sources and it was perhaps some indication of the good
reputation of the project within the local community that the
largest single source of referrals came from within that community
itself - from clients who referred the project to friends, rela-
tives and neighbours whose homes needed decoration and from potential clients who approached the project having heard of its work.
The second largest source was the local office of the DHSS whose

inspectors were so impressed by the standard of the project's work
when visiting their own clients that they began to refer some of
them to the OPDP.

From the point of view of the youngsters themselves there were
perhaps four broad areas which attracted their considerable approval. First, the level of pay was substantially higher than many
of them had been used to and was generally accepted amongst the
project's organisers to be one of the main reasons for the comparatively few voluntary departures from the project's work-force.
Second, the level of supervision, with only a brief daily visit
from a supervisor, attracted a good deal of approval as the youngsters appreciated being left alone with their work while having re-
course to advice and assistance at regular intervals when needed.
Many of the project's young workers identified intrusive levels of
supervision as the main reason for their dislike of work prior to
the OPDP. Third, the job content itself was perhaps the single
most important aspect of the work which attracted the youngsters;
the fact that they had created the finished product themselves and
were able to see, and often be complimented upon, the results of
their own efforts. Obviously this was related to the degree of
supervision which permitted (indeed was obliged to permit) the
youngsters to perform tasks in very much their own way using their
own initiative with only occasional intervention and instruction.
Finally, a fourth and interrelated aspect which won their approval
was the fact that the project dealt directly with their own community. Again their personal satisfaction was heightened since the
results of their efforts were not only immediately apparent in
terms of a redecorated room or flat but also because it was for
the benefit of an old person or someone else in need who was on
hand personally to voice their thanks and confirm the youngsters'
role as important and valuable workers. In brief, the source of
the youngsters' enthusiasm for the OPDP lay essentially in the extent to which it reproduced unskilled wage labour (the extent to
which it was a 'real job') in a particularly attractive manner –
it was ironic that the OPDP probably offered the most interesting,
fulfilling and well-paid employment that many of the youngsters
would ever experience.

Thus, despite adopting a low profile in the community and being
obliged to refrain from competition in the commercial arena, the
OPDP established a handsome reputation in the community, performed
an invaluable service for many of its most vulnerable members and
accommodated otherwise unemployed youngsters in so doing. By the
end of 1978 when it finally folded with the end of JCP nationally,
it had completed the redecoration of over 420 homes and throughout
its lifetime constantly had at least one month's advance bookings.

THE OPDP AS A JCP SCHEME: MSC GUIDELINES INTO PRACTICE

To assess the extent to which the OPDP promoted the formal objectives of JCP requires that they be identified in the first instance.
They have been concisely summarised: 'The main aim of the programme
is to provide temporary worthwhile jobs of social value, at the
appropriate local wage rate, for people who would otherwise be

unemployed and who would benefit from such work' (Department of
Employment, 1977, p.211).

The goal seems quite simple - the provision of temporary, gainful and useful employment for the otherwise unemployed. The following, however, attempts to integrate the programme's liberal
generalities through particular experience, to examine their implementation in practice in an economy in crisis and to dismantle
their logic in a competitive and antagonistic labour market. The
realisation of JCP goals were always threatened by more than mere
technical, administrative or logistical considerations and the OPDP
as a JCP scheme was essentially characterised by the sharp contradictions which marked the transition from formal guidelines to
actual practice and which can best be illuminated by reference to
those two key elements in JCP provision - assistance for 'people ...
who would benefit' and the creation of 'temporary worthwhile jobs
of social value'.

ASSISTANCE FOR 'PEOPLE ... WHO WOULD BENEFIT'

Who were these people and how would they benefit? The aim was
substantially to evacuate the unemployment register, but from the
very beginning JCP schemes were intended for very specific target
groups in the unemployed population: 'In operating the programme
the government asked the Commission to pay particular attention to
the needs of unemployed young people aged 16-24 years and the over
50s and to take account of training requirements where appropriate'
(MSC, 1979a, p.50).

Thus, two particular age groups were given priority - 16- to 24-
year-olds and the over 50s. In fact, as a JCP scheme the OPDP was
heavily populated by 16- to 19-year-olds and never did employ a
single over 50-year-old. Furthermore, the 16- to 24-year-old target
group obviously comprised young females (whom the MSC recognised as
experiencing especially severe problems) as well as males, but again
the OPDP only ever employed one young woman throughout its lifespan.
Of course the absence of older workers and young females was hardly
surprising since the OPDP was quite explicitly formed in response
to the predicament of young unemployed males in the Oldfield area.
It was obviously never the intention that each JCP scheme should
necessarily employ members of each target group in some notional
proper proportion but that somehow individual schemes would cater
for particular groups just as the OPDP accommodated young males.
But the question arises as to what extent the JCP initiative in
general could ever have been expected to reach specifically its
young female and over 50-year-old target groups in principle?

With regard to older workers, JCP wage rates were at least nominally equated with local rates of pay but subject to a maximum
rate which was adjusted over the years of its operation but which
was nevertheless always less than, for example, everage weekly
earnings in manufacturing industry. Furthermore, JCP's flat-rate
payment system precluded shift and overtime payments so that rates
of pay were not only considerably less than those which many older
workers were accustomed to but may also have been little more than
they received in unemployment and supplementary benefit. In addi-

tion, the nature of work available or quickly mobilised, labour
intensive JCP schemes could quite simply be intrinsically unattractive to older, experienced and perhaps skilled workers with particular work habits and practices acquired over decades of wage
labour. Despite a quite explicit prioritisation, only 7 per cent
of all JCP participants were aged over 50 (see MSC, 1979a, p.51).

With regard to young women, the MSC itself has offered its own
telling observations on their participation in JCP schemes:

> Many JCP jobs are of a manual nature - for example general
> labouring on construction or environmental improvement acti-
> vities - and *this has resulted in* 76% of entrants in 1976
> being male. However this overall figure disguises the grad-
> ual increase in the proportion of women or girls employed from
> 18% in the first quarter, to 20%, 26% and 28% in each of the
> succeeding quarters. This is partly *a reflection of the growth
> in non manual and clerical types of project* which may take
> longer in preparation and planning to initiate (Department of
> Employment, 1977, p.214, my emphasis).

Thus, as far as the MSC was concerned it was the 'nature' of
the work made available through JCP schemes which 'resulted in'
a small proportion of young women being involved in them. Clearly
the MSC saw it as no part of its function to challenge the sexual
division of labour and, indeed, reinforced and reproduced it in
identifying female participation in JCP schemes as 'partly a reflection of the growh in non manual and clerical types of project'.
The OPDP's only female worker was, in fact, an administrative assistant and no woman was ever employed in the apparently exclusively
and obviously male preserve of painting and decorating. There was
a quite explicit and oppressive assessment of 'women's work' here
which informed the JCP provision and, in this instance, was used to
'explain' their underrepresentation on JCP schemes - female participation rates on JCP nationally was always only around 25 per cent.
(See Department of Employment, 1977, p.214.)

But in refining the profile of JCP's target groups there was originally one further criterion to supplement those of age and sex in
identifying 'people ... who would benefit': 'Unemployment is destructive to any person. It is at its most destructive with young
school leavers, whom the discouragement of failure to get a job may
permanently alienate from the world of work and from society' (MSC,
1976b, p.22).

The significance of first-time job seekers in the stable reproduction of the labour force over time is discussed elsewhere (see
chapter 9). Their critical, fragile relationship to the means of
production, and not least the political implications of a severely
ruptured induction into work, was clearly realised by the MSC but
in this context and from its inception the OPDP tended to operate
with a very particular, albeit informal, contrary staffing policy.
Although it was always staffed by youngsters who displayed the
lowest levels of formal academic achievement and who had left
school at the earliest possible opportunity, they were nevertheless
invariably youngsters who had at least some degree of labour market
experience behind them. There was a marked preference for this
type of youngster rather than the school-leaver or first-time job
seeker which emerged from a quite distinct recruitment and selection

policy operated by the project co-ordinator. He not only favoured
youngsters with some acquaintance with basic work routines and disciplines but also preferred those with specific background in the
painting and decorating trade. Consequently, throughout the period
of its operation the vast majority of the project's employees were
those with appropriate experience, often as lapsed apprentices and,
ideally, as former apprentices in the painting and decorating trade.
   There were basically two reasons underlying the policy as operated by the project co-ordinator. First, the work of the OPDP was
such that it dealt directly with the public and entailed a certain
degree of domestic disruption and inconvenience for clients. If employees were unreliable, ill-disciplined or in any way abused their
relationship with clients, then the project co-ordinator argued that
the successful operation of the project would inevitably be jeopar-
dised. There had been a time in the project's history when some
'at risk' youngsters (e.g. those with a criminal record) had been
recruited but they had either invited dismissal through quite in-
tolerable behaviour in clients' homes or else voluntarily left the
OPDP through their own inability or reluctance to persevere with
the job. In any event, he argued the recruitment of especially 'at
risk' youngsters certainly did not contribute to the stability of
the project's work-force - a stability which he maintained was crucial to the success of the project.
   Second, because the project depended on informal and unorthodox
means of referral to clients, its reputation in the community was
held to be of paramount importance. This was felt to be reflected
not only by its treatment of clients but also in the quality of the
work which it undertook. Because for reasons of cost, all painting
and decorating was performed using the cheapest and most basic of
materials, the project co-ordinator felt that the standard of work-
manship must be of the highest order. If it were otherwise, not
only would the operation of the project be hopelessly complicated
by constant return trips to unsatisfied clients to repair unsatis-
factory jobs, but also the reputation of the project would suffer
and invaluable sources of referral inevitably dwindle.
   For the above reasons the project co-ordinator emphasised that
it was crucial that prospective employees should therefore not only
be aware of their responsibilities in clients' homes (and that a
history of labour market experience best illustrated their suit-
ability in this respect) but also that they should display some
degree of job specific skills. Both these attributes were felt to
be crucial to the project, dealing as it did with the public and
depending as it did on its good reputation within the community.
   Although the MSC clearly identified school-leavers as a priority
group it was quite clear that the OPDP, for example, operated in
practice a quite contradictory recruitment policy in order to
'cream off' certain more attractive unemployed applicants. Indeed,
given the project's priorities it is hard to see how it could have
operated otherwise in maintaining its efficiency, reputation and
credibility in the community. Consequently, it was the more experienced, more mature and more reliable who tended to be favoured
and this preference was more than just a reflection of an individual's level of technical expertise or familiarity with job specific skills but arose from an assessment of 'maturity' and 'charac-

ter' in precisely discriminating against those particular forms of young labour who were at least nominally a prime MSC target.

There was an irresolvable contradiction here and the MSC was inevitably compromised by its desire to mobilise quickly numerous labour intensive schemes nationwide, on the one hand, and to do so through the agency of voluntary sponsors, on the other. Crucially, to attract sponsors in any number and seduce them into participation, the MSC had to recognise that the costs to potential sponsors were not limited simply to pay packets, insurance contributions and so forth. For JCP sponsors, like any orthodox employer, there were certain forms of labour, certain 'types' of worker who incurred costs in excess of the normally budgeted variety - costs related to inexperience, unreliability and ill-discipline which any employer with any sensitivity to the competitive demands of the market would not seek to bear. Consequently, sponsors had to be accorded certain prerogatives in the screening and recruitment (and dismissal) of the unemployed.

The OPDP, for example, did employ youngsters who had left school with very few, if any, qualifications and who had largely drifted through the labour market without completing any kind of formal skills training. But if they were technically unskilled and correspondingly 'at risk' they were not the most 'at risk', the most inexperienced or unskilled of unemployed early school-leavers. They did have certain attributes and qualities which, fortuitously, the OPDP was looking for and which recommended them to it. And although it may have been sound policy for the OPDP, the exercise of any preference, the very act of screening began by definition to discriminate, to promote some and marginalise others and mitigated against that very group which the MSC had euphemistically termed 'the least able'.

Crucially, 'the least able' are not inherently so but defined thus by a competitive system of labour market entry and to replicate it within the JCP initiative by conceding selective recruitment not only perpetuated 'free' market antagonisms but also ensured the reproduction of competitive divisions amongst the unemployed. As long as orthodox employer-based prerogatives remain then it becomes futile to try to promote specific target groups marginalised by the prior exercise of those same prerogatives. For 'the least able', any selective recruitment policy has discrimination as its corollary and it is hard to see how the 'opportunities' thrown up by JCP were of a 'new kind' for them. The extent to which they could expect to benefit from JCP provision was the extent to which individual sponsors might voluntarily emerge who were willing to accommodate otherwise unattractive groups in contriving forms of 'sheltered' employment to deflect the exigencies of the 'normal' labour market. This, of course, required a particularly resourceful type of sponsor and represented such a commercially perverse activity that it was not surprising that the lack of private capital involvement remained one of the key features of the JCP initiative (less than 5 per cent of all provision was located in the private sector - see Department of Employment, 1977).

Given the institutional imperative of the first generation of 'special measures' (i.e. to get the unemployed off the register), it is easy to appreciate the equivalence of each JCP placement as

far as the MSC was concerned. Statistically, each placement was
precisely the same as another and the JCP guidelines had to ensure
a substantial evacuation of the register. But the necessarily
vaguely formulated and administered criteria regarding 'people ...
who would benefit', on the one hand, did not translate easily into
specific target groups identified by age, sex and (lack of) qualifications, on the other. The MSC, unable to compel or direct
sponsors in recruitment, other than within broad parameters, could
not promote specific groups and was consequently incapable of reaching them other than by chance, by the fortuitous appearance of
suitably inclined sponsors. It is only by collapsing 'the least
able' into the unemployed until they became synonymous that the MSC
can claim to have accommodated them to any significant extent and
by then, of course, the notion of specific unemployed target groups
has vanished.

    However, even though it could not reach its target groups and
'people ... who would benefit' came to mean largely the young, male
unemployed, JCP, through schemes such as the OPDP, did succeed in
placing large numbers of otherwise unemployed people in various
forms of temporary work - some 200,000 of them according to MSC
estimates (see MSC, 1979a, p.51). If the MSC largely failed to
accommodate its own target groups and one key element in its provision went unrealised, how successful was it with its second element, the creation of 'temporary, worthwhile jobs of social value',
and precisely how could the incumbents of those jobs expect to
'benefit'?

THE CREATION OF 'TEMPORARY, WORTHWHILE JOBS OF SOCIAL VALUE'

What sort of jobs were to be created? What was their purpose and
how would they occupy the unemployed? Although they were conceived
essentially as an alternative to unemployment they were also always
seen as a means to achieving additional ends:

    We have asked the Manpower Services Commission ... to concentrate
    on the problems of urban renewal, the centre of our great cities,
    and on minor works in housing, schools and hospitals which have
    real value to the community, and we have asked them, as far as
    possible, to arrange that the temporary jobs will be linked with
    some form of vocational training and will, where possible, be
    compatible with some form of further education (Denis Healey,
    'Financial Times', 25 September 1975).

    In the first instance it is not easy to see how JCP was really
expected to promote urban renewal and combat inner-city decline
when decades of compensatory regional and urban programmes had
failed (particularly with increasingly vicious public expenditure
cuts simultaneously exacerbating the problem). But there were
nevertheless genuine local needs which the OPDP did meet in becoming of 'real value to the community'. As already noted, the people
of Oldfield (and surrounding areas) did react with remarkable enthusiasm to the presence of the OPDP in their midst. Despite being
obliged to keep a low profile and operate on the commercial peri-
phery, the OPDP's reputation was such that word of mouth and informal networks became its prime source of referrals. There was

obviously a real social need to be met here and the OPDP throughout its lifetime performed a valuable function for many old folk
and others unable to meet the full market cost of redecorating
their homes.

Although the OPDP was unequivocally of real service to the community and JCP offered a real opportunity for such schemes to develop, it must be pointed out that to render JCP 'temporary' in
perpetuating the fragile myth of a 'cyclical' problem did nothing
in the longer term to meet the permanent needs of many people such
as those in Oldfield. Their problems are numerous and enduring,
indeed structural, and were only briefly, partially and fortuitously alleviated by one particular painting and decorating project
which happened to be sensitive to at least some of them. The OPDP
has disappeared but the needs and problems remain.

Of course there is a sense in which JCP itself never really disappeared (except in name) but rather became amalgamated into the
second generation of 'Special Measures' which began to emerge in
1978. Following the Holland Report, the Special Temporary Employment Programme (STEP) was explicitly modelled on JCP in catering
for the older, long-term unemployed and although there was nothing
in YOP precisely equivalent to JCP there were elements (such as the
new community service schemes) which, together with STEP, offered
the opportunity to sustain provision of projects of 'real value to
the community'. But community service schemes only offered around
12 per cent of YOP work experience places in 1978-9, only around
17 per cent in 1979-80 and were only ever intended to form some 20
per cent of YOP work experience provision in the first instance
(see MSC, 1980a, p.9 and MSC, 1977a, p.48). Moreover, with regard
to STEP even MSC admits that it is 'very small in relation to the
overall size of the problem' (MSC, 1980a, p.14), that 'the rising
unemployment will highlight the inadequacy of the scale of the
present programme' (MSC, 1980b, p.30) and, crucially, that public
expenditure cuts have fundamentally eroded its JCP inheritance:
'Renewal of schemes will no longer be straightforward or automatic....
However socially desirable it may be to continue a scheme this is a
secondary consideration....(The same can be said of course for an
initial application)' (MSC, 1979b, my emphasis).

If schemes of 'real value to the community' were originally of
prime importance but have since been relegated to a minor role (and
even then have failed to play it) then what has replaced them in the
massive (and continuing) expansion which has followed the Holland
Report? The report itself presaged an important shift in the nature
of provision which can be detected in its account of JCP's contribution:

> There have been criticisms of the quality of some Job Creation
> Programme projects. Many projects, however, are of excellent
> quality and the overall standard has been rising. *Moreover the*
> *extent to which the Job Creation Programme helps to cultivate*
> *good working habits among young people and gives them experience*
> *in work discipline has tended to be undervalued* (MSC, 1977a,
> p.28, my emphasis).

This heralded a critical realignment of MSC priorities. From the
creation of 'worthwhile jobs of social value' through JCP the MSC
had moved to the provision of 'a range of opportunities for

unemployed young people, the aim of which is to improve their
employability and help them find suitable permanent employment'
(MSC, 1977b, p.37) through YOP. And the shift signals more than
just a change in vocabulary. The original JCP initiative at least
crudely acknowledged that the problem was a lack of jobs and sought
to alleviate it through the creation of alternative, socially useful
work. The Holland Report and subsequent measures did something
quite different. They began, however insidiously, to propose an
explanation. The unemployed are no longer so numerous because of
an obvious lack of jobs but because they are inadequate and need
to 'improve their employability', they need to 'cultivate good
working habits' and gain 'experience in work disciplines'. If a
massive spending programme was to be defended politically and institutionally, the MSC had to begin to offer explanations and amplify
causes rather than simply expensively accommodating effects and this
process is discussed at length elsewhere in this volume (see chapter
5). But for the purposes of this contribution, to illustrate the
potential of JCP denied by its demise (and largely unrealised in
its enfeebled YOP/STEP mutation) and to convey the absurd and oppressive logic of post-JCP developments the following quote will suffice:

> In the 'light-box' assembly workshop, a similar pattern of work
> has been established. Here trainees construct, wire and test
> equipment, then package it and write the accompanying advice
> notes. The organisation is tight and efficient, and a convinc-
> ing assembly regime is produced. When the light boxes reach
> their destination in the main college building they are dis-
> mantled and their components fed back for assembly (Further Edu-
> cation Curriculum Review and Development Unit, 1978, p.29).

The above emerges from a review of 'best practice' in further
education provision for the young unemployed and captures the material and social consequences of present MSC strategy. The shift from
JCP work to YOP work experience recognised that for the unskilled
unemployed, job specific skills could be acquired quickly and easily
on the job (if and when they found one) and that unskilled wage
labour is largely easily reproduced at the technical/cognitive level.
But it is correspondingly boring, meaningless, intellectually and
emotionally stultifying and consequently extremely demanding. The
'skills' required here were not job specific but of the 'generic'
variety and this is the territory which YOP has colonised with its
'Social and Life Skills' modules and their chilling emphasis on
'resisting provocation', 'coping' and 'taking orders' (see MSC,
1976c and chapter 9). There is a stark realism in the light-box
assembly workshop which is both revealing and virulently oppressive.
Its 'trainees' are there to work diligently and consistently but
without purpose (other than that they should continue to do so) and
the 'convincing assembly regime' is stripped of and precludes the
social or community utility which JCP may never have guaranteed but
at least offered. The waste of resources and individual and collective potential that unemployment represents is responded to here,
not by the production of socially useful goods or services, but by
the bizarre creation of an elaborate 'training' programme in con-
trived imitation of a production line consistently regurgitating
dummy goods for fake customers. At the very least the OPDP was providing a real service for real people with genuine needs - and accommodating the unemployed in doing so.

This is not to say, however, that JCP was visited upon the unemployed and directed towards projects of social value out of some wholly bountiful impulse on the part of the state. It was never intended that the unemployed should be just temporarily accommodated (however usefully) and the 'training' for 'employability' which suffuses YOP was anticipated by the vague, qualified but nonetheless indicative references to off-the-job training and other forms of further education for JCP employees. For if JCP was not to be dismissed as a mere palliative offering short-term remedial 'make-work' projects for the unemployed, it had to have some ostensibly positive function, some 'worthwhile' component. Thus, over thirty years after the 1944 Education Act had originally proposed it, the MSC disinterred the day-release principle (hitherto restricted to apprentices and white-collar trainees) and JCP employees were to be induced to self-improvement and personal development through an exposure to 'some form of vocational training ... compatible with some form of further education'.

Thus the OPDP staff were dispatched to a local technical college where, in fact, the overwhelming response from all quarters was that the episode (a one-month block course in the painting and decorating trade) had been totally unsuccessful. The project's supervisors felt that the youngsters did not benefit formally in any way but instead regarded the event as a sort of holiday, showing no signs of discipline or inclination to study. The course tutors in turn reported the youngsters as unresponsive, unruly and practically impossible to control, let alone teach. The youngsters themselves regarded the whole exercise as unnecessary and irrelevant.

The course was clearly entirely inappropriate in a number of ways. It was classroom based and consequently highly unattractive to a group of youngsters who had left school at the earliest possible opportunity intent on never returning to the classroom again. It was geared to aspects of the painting and decorating trade (such as the chemical composition of paints and dyes) which they found obscure and far removed from day-to-day practice. The end result was that, bored and antagonised by college-based formalities, they became fractious and resentful.

It is easy to see why the OPDP's off-the-job training with its classroom orientation and the smack of schooling was wholly unattractive to the youngsters who (sporadically) attended it. Arguably, their rejection of it was altogether justified. Its value as a 'worthwhile' interlude was easily calculated, especially given the observations of one of the OPDP supervisors: 'Painters and decorators aren't ten a penny round here - they're *fifty* a penny. Why do you think I'm working for the OPDP?' If experienced, skilled workers were so abundant and available for work, what were the chances of a group of unskilled youngsters whose only claim to 'vocational training' was a one-month block course? Their assessment was well founded as they understandably saw it as wholly inadequate. But, crucially, it is not enough to dismiss their behaviour as merely disruptive nor to account for the episode as symptomatic of insensitive provision for particularly demanding youngsters. The OPDP staff were not just being wantonly unco-operative nor was the MSC merely struggling nobly to respond to their 'needs'.

With regard to the former, recent studies of the schooling of

working-class boys and their transition to work have illustrated
the integrity and intransigence of their resistance to and eager
escape from the state education system (see Willis 1977, and
Corrigan 1979). For these youngsters unskilled wage labour is not
something which befalls them from which they must be rescued or
diverted but something which they actively favour and collectively
celebrate. The significance for the OPDP in particular and post-
school provision within MSC interventions in general is that their
transition to work is impelled by a profound antagonism towards
statutory schooling in all its institutional forms. For them the
costs of the pointless conformism and daily self-denial involved in
the rigours and disciplines of formal education mean real and immediate sacrifices and deprivations; the loss of gratifications
and diversions which they know offers not even the flimsiest guarantee of an occupational 'pay off'.

In so doing they effectively (though not self-consciously) see
through the false premise or empty promise of formal educational/
vocational achievement in a labour market characterised by a competitive system of entry. For if they were all to complete 'some
form of vocational training' (just as if they were all to gain CSE,
O or A levels) then that would not offer any assurance of a job
(even MSC has to recognise this) but simply 'up' the terms of competition for whatever jobs were available - jobs whose number and
nature are determined by the 'pull' of the market and not by the
'push' of the attributes (educational or otherwise) of their potential incumbents. Even if they all emerged from 'some form of further education' in a paper snowstorm of certificated achievement,
the journey from barrow boy to captain of industry is taken only
by the occasional individual and is not one which can ever be taken
collectively by their class as a whole. Whatever the slips and
slides of individual mobility, they are collectively anchored at
the bottom of the occupational hierarchy, with the possibility of
real upward mobility so remote as to be insignificant.

For these youngsters, self-development, job satisfaction and
careers are myths which have no purchase within unskilled manual
labour so that it becomes futile to exercise spurious preferences
or engage in agonising decisions about undifferentiated options.
Consequently, if the OPDP youngsters regarded 'what do you want to
be?' as a profoundly irrelevant question, the MSC has simply stopped
asking their YOP successors. Even in the full clamour of the MSC
response its recommendation of orthodox further education and vocational training as the path to upward mobility and the salvation of
the unskilled unemployed was always tentative, encouraged 'where
possible' and 'where practicable' until the second generation of
'special measures' abandoned these traditional totems of the meritocracy altogether. By the late 1970s the recession was deepening and
the new 'realism' of the MSC ironically told the young unemployed
what many of them knew only too well - that the labour market was a
competitive and antagonistic place and that particular qualities
and 'skills' were needed to survive and endure it.

These qualities, which the 'hidden curriculum' of orthodox skills
training had recognised and reproduced for years (discipline, relia-
bility, dependency), were rediscovered by MSC and refurbished as the
new 'Social and Life Skills'. The emphasis now is no longer on

vocational training but on vocational preparation, on those 'generic' transferable skills which are to be applied to work whatever its nature (see chapter 9). There is a marked shift here from the progressivism of careers guidance, counselling a critical awareness and the active exercise of preferences in occupational choice, to the dead hand of 'Social and Life Skills' training enervating resistance and promoting quiescence. There is, for example, nowhere in the Holland Report (or other 'special measures' literature) where the working-class young are exhorted, however rhetorically, to a 'career' or referred to 'ambition' or any other elements of the social democratic repertoire so comfortably sustained during the years of ostensible full employment. The emphasis now, and with particular respect to 'the least able', is on perspiration not aspiration.

Yet crucially, if the MSC and young unskilled workers both realise that there is an array of 'skills', certain abilities and attributes which sustain the young in manual wage labour this does not mean that there is a shared understanding of them. On the contrary, what the former promotes the latter most certainly does not practise. All the experience of the OPDP with unskilled young workers suggests that MSC emphasis, however sophisticated or versatile, on 'Social and Life Skills', the inculcation of work disciplines, 'proper' attitudes or more 'committed' conceptions of working life do more than cruelly distort the reality of unskilled wage labour for many working-class youngsters; they also assault the integrity of their response to it.

For many youngsters in Oldfield, and others like them, anticipating careerless occupations and holding low expectations of work, any perspective which places emphasis on commitment, discipline and other work related 'skills' is more than irrelevant; it actually inverts and challenges those characteristics and attributes which sustain many working-class youngsters in wage labour. Their investment is in a marginal commitment, in ill-discipline, in 'messing about' and 'having a laugh' which for them colour an otherwise oppressive working day. Although voluntary early school-leavers collude in their own drift through the most insecure, demanding forms of wage labour, many of them do so with a compensatory array of skills, strategies, insights and penetrations developed during their compulsory schooling. By the time they enter the labour market, many working-class youngsters have already fashioned their own modes of deflection, resistance and survival and honed work-related skills irrepressibly antagonistic to the MSC variety. Ironically, any institutionalised attempt at transmitting 'Social and Life Skills' is thus confronted by the very same 'generic' qualities it seeks to inculcate (resourcefulness, self-reliance, opportunism) but mobilised in resistance to, rather than mechanistically out of, any statutory initiative.

Within the 'special measures', as within compulsory schooling, developmental attempts to adjust their conception of 'proper' labour market behaviour and promote means-ends schemes of advancement through 'application' and 'commitment' will not be well met and are certainly inappropriate when considering the labour market operators with whom the OPDP was concerned. They did not represent fertile soil for the sowing of the seeds of 'vocational preparation'

or 'Social and Life Skills' as currently conceived for, quite
simply, they knew better and this is the reality which the latest
MSC emphasis on 'generic' skills both distorts and offends.

They have a 'knowledge', fractional and incomplete but none the
less incisive, which sees better than any formal agency the real
state of their potential labour market and the real content and
determinants of their post-school careers. They know better than
any formal account that collectively they are destined for the lowest reaches of the occupational hierarchy. They know better than
any 'Social and Life Skills' tutor the demeaning nature of the job
opportunities available to them and the real bankruptcy of the cognitive and intellectual satisfactions within them. They know
better than any employer that repeated job changing and a marginal approach to intrinsically boring and meaningless wage labour
indicates no profligate irresponsibility but a sane response to a
labour market which for them is bereft of positive intrinsic satisfactions.

The interventions of MSC, however liberal, radical or reactionary
they may be viewed in principle, will thus inevitably struggle.
They must combat the intransigence of that which their programmes
implicitly recognise and strain to colonise - resistance. The unemployed are not simply so many of Pavlov's dogs metaphorically
salivating in response to the MSC stimulus. They do not live in
an experimental vacuum but have access to experience and forms of
knowledge and meaning available from particular class and cultural
formations which may be hostile, indifferent or politically opposed
to the thrust of MSC initiatives and understandings. The OPDP was
thus heavily populated with youngsters whose understanding of its
value, of its 'worthwhile' potential did not extend to an assimilation of off-the-job training on a one-month block course, just
as there remain youngsters whose understanding of YOP does not extend to the 'opportunity' to acquire the sorts of 'skills' in which
MSC currently traffics.

SOME CONCLUDING REMARKS

Given the nature of the inner-city labour market, the structure
of occupational opportunities and their experiences during their
schooling, it is not surprising that many youngsters such as those
who were with the OPDP do not tend to 'career' or 'commitment' in
their post-school performances. Their involvement has traditionally been with the immediate, with short-term expediency and the
maximisation of benefits latent within their immediate predicament,
i.e. quite literally making the best of a bad job.

Most unskilled jobs are the same and largely have nothing to
commend them as inherently 'worthwhile' activities - though certain sources of satisfaction can be found and these enclaves are
highly prized as primary sources of day-to-day diversion - 'good
mates', 'getting around', 'perks'. Indeed, in examining the operation of the OPDP we can see that in submitting to MSC overtures
they were able to accrue some net benefit from their participation -
notably good levels of pay, interesting manual work, a sense of
their useful productive capacity and minimal, unobtrusive levels of
supervision.

Conversely there were areas which attracted considerable dis-
approval from the youngsters. First, as we have seen, the attempt
at off-the-job training was as remarkable for its unpopularity as
its brevity. Also the project was run on a quasi-commercial basis
and its 'code of conduct' in clients' homes, for example, was sometimes breached. Given that the staff was preselected for its
prior work experience, such happenings were infrequent but occa-
sionally elicited disciplinary action which they viewed as arbitrary and intrusive. In the case of both training and disciplinary matters, what they objected to was the element of control and
constraint and their formally impotent position in the project's
hierarchy. It was the nature of the work which was so attractive
and to which they reacted so enthusiastically, but the occasional
glimpse of the full rigour of the real, formal employer/ employee
relations that aggravated them. It was this last aspect – the inculcation of work disciplines, the promotion of work socialisation –
which could be so vigorously resisted by the OPDP's young staff and
which, of course, is currently so central to MSC provision.

Yet in practice the OPDP did have much to offer its young staff,
however temporary, as it had much to offer its clients in the community. In both spheres it offered a valuable respite from the
rigours of the marketplace which had marginalised the former and
condemned the latter to a deteriorating environment. In so doing
it adhered to Mukherjee's original advice in the MSC's first commissioned work in the mid-1970s to direct state funding more extensively towards a more comprehensive concept of 'public works':

> In any case, is job creation for the purpose of enhancing com-
> munity facilities, rather than solely in the production of sale-
> able goods so very radical? After all, traditional public
> works programmes which enjoy the sanction of time and history
> have always been undertaken to create jobs, which in turn
> created new public amenities. What is being proposed here is,
> in the first place, an enlargement of the legitimate objects
> of 'public works', and secondly, an alteration of approach to
> management systems for community oriented work deliberately
> created with the support of public funds (Mukherjee, 1974,
> p.65).

He went on to talk about the 'widening of job creation for the
purpose of producing public goods (as distinct from those produced
in response to market demand)' (ibid., p.65) and yet we now have
a massively enlarged programme of publicly funded provision whose
development has been characterised by a marked shift away from the
concept of 'public works' towards an emphasis on the private sector and on subsidising the recruitment of young workers to such
areas of private capital as can be seduced into accommodating
them. While we are assured that 'area staff remain constantly
alert for any possible misuse of the scheme' (MSC, 1980a, p.9),
it is easy to see, even its perfectly 'proper' practice, which
party enjoys the balance of power. In 1979-80 some 63 per cent of
all MSC youth opportunities provision lay in the private sector
and over 90 per cent of private sector involvement consisted of
Work Experience on Employers' Premises (WEEP) schemes (see MSC,
1980a, pp. 9 and 11). While it makes sound commercial sense for
capital to use WEEP as a form of cheap labour and an opportunity

to screen potential workers for six MSC-subsidised months, it is
clear that the 'special measures' have come a long way from providing 'jobs of real value to the community'. They are now more
explicitly subjugated to the commercial arena, to the 'needs' of
industry than ever before. While there remains the element of resistance amongst its young 'trainees' (as they are now called) the
MSC will always struggle to achieve its more ambitious and oppressive aims (the dissemination of 'Social and Life Skills'), but
it has certainly made great advances towards them in closing the
spaces opened by JCP and interring the principle of 'public works'
offering jobs of 'social value' which held so much potential for
communities such as Oldfield.

Chapter 8

CLIENT RESPONSE TO THE YOUTH OPPORTUNITIES PROGRAMME

Howard Williamson

INTRODUCTION

The Youth Opportunities Programme (YOP) is frequently perceived and presented as an homogenous programme, with the implication that its operation and impact is uniform throughout. Even those who are quite aware of the distinctive elements of YOP often stumble into the same trap when they say 'one point about YOP is that'. Such a blanket categorisation just cannot be attempted.

YOP is a diverse programme enveloping, amongst other things, college-based courses of varying content and duration, project and placement schemes, training workshops, and work experience with employers. Some schemes are overtly selective and others may be selective as a result of preselection by the Careers Service; many schemes, in contrast, have an 'open door' policy. Some staff on schemes are essentially 'professional' people while others may be described personal histories of manual/industrial work and may be described as 'working class'. Some schemes emphasise the 'social' and train-ing elements of YOP; others simply get on with work, and attempt to provide a working environment and to establish good working habits in trainees. The point is that no two schemes - whether they are project based, community service, or whatever - are likely to be the same. The staff of particular projects within even the same type of scheme will have different conceptions of purpose, and will attach different weights to selected aspects of the broad substance available within YOP.

The formal rationale of YOP was to develop an integrated system of training, education and work for young people out of work. It was to bring together under one umbrella the different strands of earlier government provision, and was an overt attempt to break into the vicious circle within which untrained, unqualified and unskilled young people were unable to get work because they had no experience and unable to get experience because they had no job. YOP, therefore, was a measure designed to provide this experience and was conceived as a 'constructive alternative to unemployment' (MSC, 1977a, p.33). While recognising the possible danger of older generations determining what constituted relevant oppor-tunities for young people, the Holland Report - the catalyst for

the programme - maintained that although YOP could not offer a
job, it could be 'responsive to the differing needs of unemployed
young people', meeting their personal needs and giving a 'competitive edge to young people in the labour market' (MSC, 1977a,
p.43). The programme, then, claimed to respond to the stated
needs of the unemployed young.

Other interpretations of the rationale underpinning the development of such extensive (and expensive) state intervention are
available and have been discussed elsewhere in this volume (see
also Williamson, 1980). Briefly, these include the possibility
that YOP is no more than a cosmetic measure to conceal the true
level of youth unemployment and that it is a new version of social
control occasioned by a panic about 'idle youth' - Frith (1978a)
argues that state intervention for the young unemployed is a form
of capitalist labour control. There is also the suggestion that
it is designed to fulfil a need to socialise young people into
work; and finally that YOP may be doing no more than redistri-
buting job opportunities within the same social group by, for
example, making YOP trainees more competitive in the labour market
than their peers who do not participate in the programme (see
Williamson, 1979).

More crucially, though, it is useful to examine how the staff
of schemes explain the purpose of the programme. Once again, we
must not take YOP staff to be an homogeneous group. Nevertheless,
as I have suggested, they may be allotted to two general categories. First, there are those who may be described as the 'professional' managers and supervisors. These are individuals who,
broadly speaking, have an 'academic/social work' background - for
example, graduates, social workers or teachers. In addition,
there are individuals for whom working on YOP is 'the next best
thing to youth work'. The reasons for their involvement in YOP are
diverse. Some may see it as a challenge away from conventional
social work or teaching; others may themselves have been the 'victims' of receding employment opportunities and see YOP as a new
avenue for professional work. This category is predominantly
young and female. Second, there are those who have industrial
working backgrounds. Again, they also may have been victims of
the employment situation, having been made redundant and unable
to find work. Alternatively they may be relatively financially
secure (as a result of army pensions, redundancy payments and so
on) and see YOP as a new challenge involving greater diversity
than conventional manual or managerial work. It is a challenge
which some take up despite (in their view) the low pay because they
have other resources to supplement this income or because they can
use their skills and 'their' lads (i.e. trainees) to make extra
cash by doing 'foreigners' in the informal economy. (It has been
argued that the relationship between the formal and informal economies is a constantly changing one; in times of economic depression, both the supply and demand for certain forms of labour may
increase considerably - see Gershuny and Pahl, 1980.) This category tends to be older and male.

These two categories of staff have very different conceptions
of the purposes of YOP, though both may make similar assumptions
about the kind of young person who participates in the programme.

The former, however, place far greater emphasis on the social
aspects of YOP, particularly social and life skills, personal
help, support and counselling: their purpose is to ease young
people into all aspects of adulthood through discussion, education
and learning about life. The latter, in contrast, play down the
value of formal social and life skills (see below) and explain
their purpose almost exclusively in terms of work: to get young
people into the habit of work, perhaps into the habits of certain
kinds of work, and to impress upon them just what is acceptable and
unacceptable in the world of work with little discussion or ques-
tioning as to why this may be so. The point that some staff see
their role as inculcating specific works skills, rather than more
generalised work-related skills, is somewhat contentious since YOP
is not intended to offer training in particular forms of work (such
as carpentry, engineering or bricklaying). Nevertheless, with
skilled or semi-skilled men as supervisors on many schemes, this
could feasibly be an unintended consequence of the programme.
Moreover, the objectives of 'working-class' staff may be realised
through the establishment of work-related skills such as turning up
on time and responding to the disciplinary practices of the workplace.

Of course, the differential targets set by 'professional' and
'working-class' staff are quite explicable in that the former
have little or limited knowledge of manual working conditions while
the latter are not (at least formally) equipped to tackle issues
involving interpersonal skills. As a result, both sieze upon those
aspects of their own work experience which they can offer confidently to young people on the programme. It is only when we turn to
the response of these young people to YOP provision that these distinct perspectives can be assessed.

It has been mentioned already that YOP was originally argued to
be a response to the stated needs and desires of the young unemployed themselves. For example:

These young people are well aware of the facts. They know that
the chances of getting a job were less than they were formerly
and that finding a job would be difficult. When it comes to
the kind of help they need, they say they are looking for help
in how to set about looking for a job and how to present themselves at an interview and they want the opportunity to learn
skills for the job they have chosen (Department of Employment,
1978).

Yet can YOP - in its many forms - be interpreted as a relevant
response? Certainly the flexibility of YOP could potentially respond to many different needs but much of the current provision
appears to be floundering in an attempt to establish practices
designed to meet both 'social' and 'employment' needs, which are
often irresolvable in the same setting since solutions at one level
tend to militate against solutions at the others. The allocation
of time, for example, to talk through personal problems conflicts
with any attempt to create a 'real' work situation. This problem
is central to the dilemmas of YOP and is discussed in more detail
below. For many trainees, however, these dilemmas are not apparent:
indeed, when asked about 'personal problems', trainees invariably
mentioned work and disciplinary issues The trainees under discus-

sion in this paper perceived YOP as very firmly located around work.
Consequently, they had clear, if misguided and inaccurate understandings of what YOP is about, and very explicit preferences for
certain types of scheme and staff.

CLIENTS' VIEWS OF THE YOUTH OPPORTUNITIES PROGRAMME

The clients' views of YOP presented in this paper are drawn from
a series of interviews with a substantial number of YOP participants in a variety of schemes in the West Midlands. The interviews,
which were mostly taped, were conducted between October 1979 and
March 1980 with young people on project-based work experience,
training workshops and community service placements. The chapter
focuses, however, on the responses of forty-five (predominantly
white) male trainees from three schemes concerned with 'traditional'
male work: carpentry, construction, painting and decorating and engineering. The experience of girls, ethnic minorities and trainees
on Work Experience on Employers' Premises (WEEP) is qualitatively
different and is not explored here in any depth.

The trainees considered in this discussion are not individuals
who should be classed as 'unemployable'. The most accurate definition of 'unemployability' is literally the inability to get and
retain work even in times of full employment. However, the label
'unemployable' is being attached increasingly to YOP trainees, with
the implication that certain personal characteristics (such as laziness, or non-acceptance of discipline) must be corrected before they
have any chance of securing a 'real' job. It is interesting that
such assumptions should have developed, since the Holland Report
was careful to note that:

> Success or failure in getting a job is often a matter of luck
> and frequently determined by factors well beyond the control
> or achievement of the individual such as the state of the
> national economy, the local industrial structure or the kind of
> preparation for work available at school. Unemployed young
> people are not failures: they are those whom others have so
> far failed (MSC, 1977a, p.33).

Yet, as we shall see, these wider factors are often ignored or
suppressed and the failure of YOP trainees to find work has been
'individualised'.

The industrial structure of the West Midlands is located around
heavy engineering, the motor industry and a vast number of small
businesses which 'service' the larger concerns. The area has, in
the past, been relatively cushioned from the effects of economic
recession, at least until recently. Therefore it does not have a
history of large-scale unemployment like other similar areas such
as Liverpool. Young people - even those with no qualifications,
minor personal handicaps or criminal records - were absorbed easily
into work in the building trade, the commercial centre or small
garages. While they may not have had a formal apprenticeship, they
gained knowledge and experience by 'serving time' and often became
recognised locally as 'skilled' as the indigenous manual population
will bear out including some of the 'working-class' supervisors:
one, when asked what his background was, replied:

I'm a brickie by trade.... I mean, before the war like, you were
a carpenter on a building, and you chased around and you followed a load of timber, and see if you could get a job, and you
couldn't get a job, and the next day you go round the same jobs
again as a bricklayer. I mean I used to stand up there and the
good bricklayers were on the corners, and you got a trowel,
you got an old trowel, and that like, and you used to wait
there, you didn't know how the bloody hell to lay a brick....
I have gone and applied for a job, you know, on a site, and they
have wanted somebody and I've gone for that job. I even went
as a marble mason once - I didn't know the first thing about it
.... I was out of work and I went up there, and I walked on the
job and a bloke said 'are you looking for somebody?' I said
'Ah, I'm looking for the foreman, like, you know. I am after
a job.' He said 'You wouldn't happen to be a marble mason would
you?' and I said 'Oh I have worked with them, I know about it
like,' and he said 'Well there is a job here for a marble mason.'
I said, 'Ah, that'll do,' I said, 'But the trouble is, my tools
are up in Stockport, I've got no tools here like." And he said,
'Oh well you can muck in and use mine' like that. Well, I mean,
you was just holding him. You saw him drilling and fixing and
all that, a few minutes and you knew how to do it, and then you
were doing it....

For many years, hard work and application were the only qualifications needed. In the last few years, however, the West Midlands
has been hit severely by the industrial recession, particularly by
the problems in the motor industry. Birmingham's unemployment
rate was 7.3 per cent in June 1980, compared to a national rate of
6.3 per cent. Following a spate of redundancies in the motor
vehicle and related industries, 48 per cent of local firms planned
to cut jobs compared to 21 per cent in December 1979 (Youth Employment Resource Unit, 1980). The employment situation, especially
for young people, is rapidly deteriorating. Vacancies registered
with the Careers Service in 1980 were down by half on the 1979
figures, while the numbers seeking work continued to rise. By February 1981, Birmingham's rate of unemployment had risen to 12.4 per
cent compared to the West Midland's rate of 11.7 per cent and a
national figure of 10 per cent. In the previous month - the annual
'trough' of youth unemployment - approaching 20 per cent of those
under 18 were unemployed.

The net effect of this rising unemployment is that the 'qualification bar' for any job creeps up the qualification ladder, leaving the least qualified young people factually, though not technically, almost 'unemployable', and certainly quite unlikely to
secure even semi-skilled work. The point which must be continu-
ally borne in mind is that in previous years their chances of getting work were reasonably good. Any 'social' disadvantage did not
necessarily handicap them in terms of employment chances.

One of the key issues in clients' responses to YOP is that unlike the staff, who may perceive YOP as offering something away
from conventional work, many of these trainees see the schemes as
presenting a new (alternative) route into conventional work. This
is especially the case for those trainees for whom traditional
avenues into 'skilled work have been blocked, both by their poor

formal educational qualifications and the trend for employers to demand higher and higher grades. In addition, there have of course been fewer and fewer opportunities for, for example, apprentice-ships.

This perspective would appear to contradict the views of many staff who would argue either that trainees are of too low a calibre to be possibly able to undertake any kind of 'skilled' work (such as bricklaying), or alternatively suggest more 'liberally' that while trainees are just 'normal kids', they are nevertheless heavily disadvantaged in the employment market as a result of deprived home circumstances or because the education system has let them down. Certainly many individual examples may be found to bear out such views. There are substantial numbers of both socially and physi-cally disadvantaged young people on YOP schemes as well as a con-siderable number classed as educationally subnormal. Furthermore, some are 'disadvantaged' because they possess criminal records. For these groups, perhaps, YOP is indeed 'better than the dole' or at least 'it keeps you off the streets'. For a further number of supposedly slightly 'higher calibre' young people, the rationale for their taking up a YOP opportunity is also that it is 'better than the dole'. Both of these groups, then, give credence to the official view that YOP is a 'constructive alternative to unemploy-ment'. (A pertinent question here, though, is whether the Pro-gramme – while shielding these groups from the harsh realities of work and unemployment – can effectively make them more competitive so that they may realise their aspirations to work, or whether it is simply deferring the time when these young people must face, and perhaps fail in, the fierce competition of the labour market.)

In this chapter, however, I wish to pursue the attitudes and assumptions of those young people who argue that YOP, for them, is more of a constructive alternative to employment. The intention is to portray a groups of trainees (who, on some schemes in parti-cular, comprise a substantial number) which in many respects does not fall easily into the categorisation of YOP trainees as somehow socially 'inadequate', culturally inept or occupationally naive (see chapter 9). Two categories which emerge quite clearly from this group are those who see YOP as a means of realising certain 'skilled' work aspirations (as I have mentioned above) and those for whom YOP is regarded as a 'cushy number'.

'MY DAD'S A CARPENTER, MY BROTHER'S A CARPENTER AND I WANT TO BE ONE':   YOP AS SKILL TRAINING

While the officialdom of YOP repeatedly mentions the term 'dis-advantage' in discussions of YOP clientele, this, in some cases at least, may be grossly misleading or even irrelevant. There is no automatic causal link between poor home backgrounds and occupa-tional failure (although it may be stronger if one ignores the pro-cesses of the 'informal' occupational world). Nor are trainees likely to agree that they are on YOP because of certain personal or environmental deficiencies which the programme is seeking to correct. On the contrary, rather than correcting supposedly negative attributes, YOP is seen by many trainees to be supple-

menting or boosting a positive attribute - that is, the desire to
learn a 'trade'.

When asked what they hope to do as a job in the future, trainees
invariably relate to the kind of work they are doing on a scheme -
'I've always wanted to be a brickie', 'I'm hoping to be an electri-
cian', and so on. Furthermore, when questioned as to why they had
come on to a particular scheme - apart from the amorphous and negative 'it's better than the dole' - trainees state that it was in
order to learn a specific form of work. (This point lies in stark
contrast to the MSC's avowal that YOP is not about specific forms
of work.) These trainees often commence a scheme under very false
impressions as to what the scheme will provide for them, and appear
to have been ill-informed by the Careers Service (or YOP staff
when they came for interview) about what YOP entails. Even the
words 'government training scheme' - which is how trainees tend
to describe YOP if they do not claim it is a job - imply (to young
people) training in skills rather than the less tangible concepts
of training for work or training for life. 'Government training
courses' within YOP are frequently conceived as a junior version
of Skill Centre training, which does equip individuals with specific skills. The title 'trainee' confirms these false assumptions,
particularly when an occupational label is appended so that trainees
present themselves as 'trainee carpenters' or 'trainee painters',
implying that after their period of 'training' they will become
fully fledged carpenters or painters.

These assumptions often lead to rapid disillusionment with the
scheme as trainees realise that the most they will be receiving
is limited training in a specific skill: 'it's no good, you don't
make your own joints', 'it's crap, you don't build walls proper'.
Nevertheless, these trainees still feel that the experience of even
doing something in the field of work to which they aspire will
improve their chances of getting a job in the same kind of work at
the end of their time on YOP. Every trainee aspiring to particular work and doing that work on a scheme was reasonably confident
of being able to get a real job in the same line. The acquisition
of basic specific work skills leads these trainees to believe that
they have a partial 'qualification' for entry into their chosen
occupational field. The trainee below at first argued that he had
learned nothing except punctuality:

HW: So you don't think you've learned much.... I mean, what
about building?

T : Oh I know how to bricklay and slab now, but it's not going
to be any good to me to learn bricklaying, is it?

HW: Why?

T : 'cos I'm, you know, I ain't trained or nothing, I can't say
I'm a bricklayer 'cos I ain't.

HW: So how does this scheme improve your chances of getting a
job?

T : It must do, mustn't it, 'cos you can say 'I've done bricklaying' and they'll give you a job then.

HW: You think they will?

T : Yeah ... well it must improve your chances anyway.

Since one of the major criticisms of YOP trainees is that they
have quite unrealistic career aspirations, and since these trainees

remained optimistic about at least partially realising their
'skilled' work aspirations, it is useful to inquire into the background of some of these trainees to establish what their aspirations and intentions were on leaving school and how and why they
came on to YOP. Some, but by no means all of the assertions
made by YOP 'experts' are borne out, especially those which suggest
that many school-leavers fail to search hard enough for a job and
that 'typical' YOP trainees would be unlikely to hold down a real
job for any length of time. Both of these assertions do appear to
be correct, but the explanations for them may differ considerably
between staff and trainees.

The apparent lack of effort made by trainees in looking for work
is often explained by the staff to be the product of laziness ('a
lot don't want to work; they have no motivation, it's very bad,
they've got no initiative') or the fact that 'these kids are better
off on the dole': 'Seeing as they're featherbedded they've got
no ambition. If they had no money they'd fight for a job.... If
you've got nothing you start to look for something. But if you
can manage you don't.'

Failure to hold down a job is similarly explained to be the
result of poor socialisation (bad manners, cheekiness), bad timekeeping and absenteeism, and, once again, laziness. One supervisor commented 'but if he hasn't been going to school regularly
and getting there early, those habits will rub off on him and he'll
still get to work late', while another observed more broadly that
'their way of life does not allow them to improve.' The staff,
then, argue that many young people simply lack the habits and
patterns to secure and keep a real job of any kind.

Trainees have a different story to tell. There is little doubt
that some YOP trainees have not looked for work and that, of those
who have worked, a number have left or been dismissed soon afterwards. These 'facts' do not, however, justify the automatic rele-
gation of all trainees to a lumpen, uneducated, unmotivated, un-
disciplined and culturally inadequate class. (And there has been
a tendency for elements of truth to dominate the character sketches
of all individuals on YOP.) In fact, the starting point for explaining these behavioural features of trainees must be their occupational aspirations and these must be set against the rapid changes
in the levels of educational qualifications required for particular
jobs and the changes in the labour market. It might, of course, be
argued that trainees' aspirations are unjustifiably high and are
exploited as a mechanism whereby trainees have a reason for doing
nothing and this enables them to rationalise away their lack of
effort in seeking work. But this argument is tangential to an examination of how trainees react to their involvement in YOP schemes.

This category of trainee seems to have left school having at
least taken two or three CSEs and hoping to get a job which would
lead them into the world of what might be broadly termed 'skilled'
work - in other words, something more than basic factory or labouring work. It may be of interest that they rarely talked of having
tried to get an apprenticeship (though some in fact left YOP to
take up one) which perhaps reflects their marginal location in the
genuinely skilled working world. Nevertheless, they saw for themselves a future of skilled or semi-skilled work in occupations such

as carpentry, engineering, painting and decorating, electrical
work and construction. A scan through any local evening newspaper
would quickly indicate a dearth of such jobs for school-leavers or
those only slightly older. The few jobs which may be available are
likely to be snapped up immediately by those better qualified than
this group. As a result, either no applications are made or, if
they are, they are met with a response of 'no vacancies' (because
the job has 'already gone') or rejection at an interview (because
more highly qualified people are available). What is important to
note about this category of young people is that despite disillusionment and boredom on the dole, their aspirations are not depressed and they 'hold out' in the hope of still realising them.
They are aware that jobs are difficult to get and that it will take
time. One boy, when asked whether he had learned anything about
'work' from older siblings, replied 'Just that it's got a lot harder
to get jobs at all ... but because of this, not to jump at the first
job offered.' Consequently they hold out and after six weeks become eligible for YOP. By this time they are 'bored' and 'fed up'
with being on the dole and are keen to find work, although they
still want appropriate work.

Alternatively, some may have decided to take a more basic, 'dead
end' manual job, often in a factory, only to become rapidly dis-
illusioned. They leave or get sacked within a few weeks, at least
overtly because they did not feel 'suited' to the job: 'I got
the boot for messing about, but I couldn't stick it there, I was
going to leave anyway.' Another trainee commented:

'I had a job about two months after leaving school but I got
the sack. I was only there about four weeks. It was in a factory, making bog rolls - the insides of 'em. It was a load of
crap (laughs). The gaffer said I was too slow but I dain't
like it anyway. I weren't going to stick there, but ... I was
just waiting for another job but he helped me to get the sack,
like ...'

A short period of unemployment makes these individuals also eligible
for YOP.

The next step is during discussion with the Careers Service,
which is either already aware or is now informed of the individual's aspirations, which appear to be somewhat unrealistic and
therefore which need to be suppressed. At the same time, the
Service seeks to respond to the individual's working interests.
These factors, in conjunction with his eligibility for YOP and
the range of options available within YOP, propel the Careers
Officer to mention the 'government training schemes' where the individual would be able to pursue his interest in carpentry, construction or whatever. This is, at first, sufficient incentive to take
up the opportunity - 'the money ain't much cop, but I'm training,
ain't I', 'I've always wanted to work outdoors. I want to do
bricklaying and this is a start.' Soon afterwards, however, the
basic nature of the training becomes apparent and the trainee finds
that it is not meeting his aspirations as much as he had hoped
after all.

Two further qualifying points need to be made. First, although
I have argued against the blanket categorisation of YOP trainees
as suffering from a vague, intangible cultural deprivation, many

trainees of the type under discussion do appear to suffer from some concrete disadvantage which may feasibly have reduced their chances of following conventional routes into work irrespective of their educational achievements and irrespective of the employment situation. Such disadvantage included criminal records, a range of minor physical 'disabilities' (partial deafness, size, asthma), and nationality (language problems) as well as the most obvious 'problem' of skin colour. Some trainees with such problems clearly felt that YOP was presenting them with a new route where these difficulties were considered irrelevant: 'you know, they don't judge you by your character or nothing like that', said an ex-Borstal boy.

Second, while officially YOP cannot offer 'skill' training to any extent (in the way that, for example, Skill Centres do), unofficially it may. This will be dependent on the type of scheme and whether it is run by 'professional' or 'working-class' staff. The latter will be equipped to meet the voiced needs of these trainees more adequately and may also be able to use informal contacts to slot trainees into jobs which relate to their aspirations. Moreover, greater rapport will develop between trainees and these 'working-class' supervisors precisely because a version of the 'teaching paradigm' (see Willis, 1977, p.62) can be upheld - trainees have come on to YOP to acquire practical knowledge that they know these supervisors possess. In contrast, 'professional' supervisors will be denigrated by them; after all, these trainees cannot see that they need 'social skills' or related training - they have come on a government training scheme in order to learn a 'trade', or at least basic but specific work skills.

Girls on community service schemes may hold a similar attitude towards 'professional' staff, since these girls are likely to aspire to 'caring' work such as nursing or child care. Therefore 'professional' staff may be seen to have the appropriate knowledge for this type of work and the 'teaching paradigm' holds, just as it does for boys and 'working-class' staff.

A 'CUSHY NUMBER':   TOLERANCE AND FLEXIBILITY

The other major category of trainees for whom YOP constitutes an alternative to employment are those who see it as a 'cushy number'. Empirically there appears to be evidence that a considerable number of trainees show little concern about looking for jobs while they are on schemes, and only really start searching when the end of their time is in sight. In fact they regard their participation in YOP as being in a real job and despite the level of the training allowance, they find the tolerance and flexibility of YOP attractive enough to remain on schemes for as long as possible.

The potential 'cushiness' of YOP is a direct consequence of the various theoretical assumptions made by officials and staff of schemes about the 'calibre' of trainees. The individualisation of employment problems creates perceptions of trainees as lacking 'employability'. This provides the justification for schemes to shift away from simply attempting to recreate a working environment in order to provide trainees with experience of a simulated working

situation. The rationale for such a shift is based upon the following argument - (a) young people come on to YOP because they lack the
'something' necessary to compete for, secure and hold down a real
job; (b) that 'something' is essentially behavioural; (c) because
of this a scheme cannot be exactly like work since this type of
individual would be sacked within a week - for absenteeism, lateness, skiving, or messing about; (d) therefore a scheme must tolerate certain transgressions of 'normal' working practice which would
not be tolerated in the real world, and only gradually develop in
trainees the 'correct' work habits which will enable them eventually
to compete for, secure and hold down employment. There is always
one additional 'exemption clause' in this argument: (e) a scheme
may have to get rid of some trainees fairly quickly and will not
succeed with all because no scheme can always 'correct' the bad
habits which have been acquired over many years through poor
socialisation by inadequate parents. Nevertheless, in a limited
time, a scheme must do its best and it is argued that a scheme
must have some level of tolerance and flexibility in order to meet
these 'needs' of the trainees. Even those schemes which formally
stress their attempt to replicate as far as possible an authentic
working environment usually operate 'looser' disciplinary practices.
    The 'diagnosis' of the problems of the young unemployed may be
an accurate one for some trainees. However, by developing and indeed institutionalising systems of tolerance (for example, a trainee
cannot be sacked from a scheme without the approval of the MSC), a
space is created in which other trainees can, in the words of supervisors, 'play the system'. YOP schemes are not usually considered
attractive because of the rate of 'pay' - it may be 'better than
the dole', but the allowance remains the central bone of conten-
tion in discussion amongst trainees. Only those trainees who
either did not have any weekly 'costs' (like payment for keep, or
bus fares) or supplemented their income in various ways (doing
'foreigners', gambling, etc.), express reasonable satisfaction with
the allowance, although for some female trainees the 'pay' may be
attractive in comparison to the rates they would get in the type of
jobs for which they are eligible, notably shop or factory work.
    The 'comforts' of YOP then, as I have suggested, lie elsewhere,
in what might be termed the 'skiving opportunities' available on
schemes but not to the same degree in work. Indeed, this is what
differentiates many schemes from real work: 'if you was in a real
job you wouldn't be dossing around', 'you know, like over our dinner
breaks they should be stricter on 'em (i.e. trainees) and pack us
up on time and that, but they don't.' Another trainee observed,
'like I shouldn't get away with half the things I get away with.
If I was at a proper job I'd have got the sack by now, know what
I mean?' Even on schemes where the pace of work is not necessarily
any slower than real work, 'skiving opportunities' still exist.
Ironically they are present in those aspects of YOP which are of
central importance to scheme organisers and staff - punctuality
and attendance. Of course, lateness and absenteeism are likely to
invoke the sanction of loss of 'wages' and many trainees do learn
to turn up on time and come to work because they need the money.
Nevertheless, not going to work, or being late - even relatively
persistently - may involve loss of pay, but does not involve loss

of 'job'. This, for some trainees, is the great appeal of YOP.
Even absenteeism does not automatically lead to loss of pay,
especially on those schemes where the staff are 'professional'
individuals who feel that there is likely to be a significant
personal problem underlying persistent absence. Penalties for
absenteeism, in their view, should only be applied once the problem has been identified and resolved. They argue that disciplinary action, such as suspension, for the presenting problem (i.e.
lateness) is simply a form of 'copping out'. The irony of this
approach, as we have seen, is that while trainees themselves
recognise and exploit these 'systems of tolerance', they are critical of them, interpreting them as laxity on the part of the staff
since they do not see them as an accurate reflection of true working practices.

One final reason why YOP may be regarded as 'cushy' is because
trainees may be working with their friends, and this may be preferred to the anticipated isolation and loneliness of work amongst
trainees who have never had a job. Some trainees may even leave
work to get on to schemes where their friends are. More often, an
unemployed teenager will seek a place on a particular scheme as a
result of a recommendation by a friend already on that scheme:

> Then I was back on the labour and there was a mate of mine who
> had started at this place. So I had a word with my mate and
> he took me down.... 'Oh', he said, 'you have a laugh and muck
> about and all this crap, and that's it,' and I thought, well it
> might keep me off the streets and that, so I might as well join.

The main instrument of specific 'awareness' of YOP remains, however,
the Careers Service, though unemployed young people may hold vague
ideas about 'government training schemes'.

RELATIONSHIPS WITH STAFF

It is now worth turning our attention to the relationship between
trainees and the staff of YOP schemes. The 'professional'/'working-
class' dichotomy is crucial to our understanding of this relationship as well as of the responses of trainees to the differential
emphasis placed by 'professional' and 'working-class' staff on particular features of YOP - for example, social skills in a formal
setting, or discipline on the job.

At the most elementary level trainees tend to like 'professional'
supervisors as individuals but not as supervisors; conversely, they
respect 'working-class' supervisors as supervisors if not as individuals. For trainees, 'professional' supervisors are friendly
and 'nice' but can offer them little in terms of concrete training.
'Working-class' supervisors are perceived by trainees to have something to offer as supervisors - perhaps a skill or contacts with
a relevant working world - and in this way the relationship bears
some resemblance to Willis's (1977) teaching paradigm - 'knowledge
for respect, guidance for control'. Willis goes on to argue that:

> Since knowledge is the rarer commodity this gives the teacher his
> moral superiority. This is the dominant educational paradigm
> which stands outside particular teachers but enables them to
> exert control legitimately upon the children. It is legitimated

in general because it provides equivalents which can enter into
other successive exchanges which are to the advantage of the
individual. The most important chain of exchanges is, of course,
that of knowledge for qualifications, qualified activity for
higher pay, and pay for goods and services. The educational
is, therefore, the key to many other exchanges (1977, p.64).
  Unlike the 'lads' in Willis's school setting, however, trainees
view this exchange as a valid one. They perceive the knowledge of
forms of work which are held by 'working-class' supervisors as
valuable; opposition and resistance develops only when they realise that this knowledge, even when imparted, is not 'training' which
has credibility in the eyes of employers (i.e. it is not training
in a skill), or if supervisors cannot activate their contacts to
secure jobs for trainees. Thus the 'teaching paradigm' falls down
(a similar example of what is perceived as 'useless' training is
found in Gleeson and Mardle's discussion of the social education
of craft apprentices (1980)). Clearly 'working-class' supervisors
are in a better position to meet trainees' desires, but various
formal requirements of YOP may prevent them from doing so. For
example, no YOP scheme can formally offer 'skill' training, nor are
staff encouraged to bypass the Careers Service to find trainees
jobs, although, of course, some do. It should also be noted that
trainees often do not recognise the importance or value of the
knowledge traded by 'professional' staff; I am not saying that it
is not useful knowledge. Nevertheless, this point takes us on to
the issue of rapport with staff and the methods of imparting social
skills.

RAPPORT AND SOCIAL SKILLS

I have suggested that while trainees may have little respect for
'professionals' as supervisors, they usually like them as people.
In contrast, 'working-class' staff as supervisors are often res-
pected both as supervisors and as people. This is a product of
the rapport developed by this type of supervisor and the trainees,
and it has implications which run counter to the trend towards the
institutionalisation and professionalisation of social and life
skills training.
  Such rapport is often only semi verbal and therefore difficult
to capture. The following example is a verbal exchange between a
supervisor and a trainee:
    S: Mick, I expect you to get stuck into some hard work today.
    I wrote a report about you last night and it wasn't very good.
    T: (indignantly) But George, I ain't done *nothing*.
    S: That's *exactly* the problem; today I want you to do *some-
    thing*.... I don't want to have to write that 'this boy will
    spend his life pulling at doors marked "Push".'
The facetious but possibly accurate reaction (especially on the
part of 'professional' supervisors) might be that a lot of trainees
cannot read! The pertinent point is that such rapport confirms and
develops the common cultural milieu of the staff and trainees in
which team effort, co-operation and loyalty is established. Furthermore, such rapport is extended on site, in the workplace or wherever

(i.e. on the job) into an amateur but none the less effective inculcation of what might be broadly termed 'social and life skills',
though few 'working-class' supervisors would recognise or describe
it as such. An impetuous racialist comment might lead to an im-
promptu discussion of race relations; the loss of a ruler might
elicit not simply 'Well you'd better find it then' (as a 'professional' supervisor might say) but a brief and incisive lecture
about the need to look after one's tools:

> You wouldn't be like that with your rule if it were yer own.
> You know how much these things cost - three pound seventy five.
> Yeah *that much*. And you need one of them for yer living. It
> gets you to work and it pays yer wages. Without one of them
> you don't get no wages. Just remember that. Look after yer
> tools.

The lecture has an effect because the trainee knows this man
is talking from his own experience, not from theory. Willis has
suggested why working-class people denigrate theory in favour of
practice and expose the 'hollowness' of theory unless it relates
directly to practical action (1977, pp.56-7). Whereas 'professional' staff may offer generalised (social) support which may
credibly help the trainee (but many trainees cannot see its relevance), 'working-class' supervisors tend to sieze upon trainees'
own self-centredness and use this to pursue a specific point which
not only stresses certain skills relevant to work but also makes
sense to the individual trainee. The example above illustrates
this quite clearly: the work skill of looking after one's tools
is not simply in the imagination of a fussy 'gaffer'; it is directly related (in the real world of work) to having money in one's
pocket.

Such interaction is not necessarily smooth. The operation of firm
discipline may be resented at first, but the very real physical
dangers of the workplace (for instance, heavy slabs on building
sites, or machinery in workshops) soon demonstrate to trainees in
a practical way the need for discipline and the unacceptability of
'messing about'. Consequently, the guidance and information
offered by 'working-class' staff is valued by, and does have an
impact, on trainees. In contrast, the presentation of sessions
on race relations, on 'behaviour at work' or on health and safety
in a sterile 'classroom situation' (and anything which does not
involve work but is neither unpaid free time is interpreted as 'like
school') is detested and generates resentment and opposition. The
lack of its direct relevance to a concrete situation militates
against its impact.

Clearly there is a problem with this kind of 'casual', informal,
'on the job' social life and skills training which relates to the
lack of definition in what 'social and life skills' actually entail.
Should it be focused primarily on work and work related issues such
as punctuality, discipline, interview techniques or form filling?
Or should it attempt to include more 'social' subjects such as
leisure, contraception or the social security system? The essence
of the question is whether the subject matter should concentrate on
preparation for employment, or whether it should also include preparation for unemployment and for life. I have argued for the efficacy of the provision of 'social skills training' by 'working-class'

staff. However, while they may be better equipped to transmit work and work-related issues more successfully to trainees, their ability to deal with more 'social' issues is more questionable. There is a real danger that in discussions of issues such as race or contraception, traditional working-class bigotry and prejudice may be confirmed.

The expectations of the trainees under consideration, however, were that YOP was exclusively to do with work. In questionably 'objective' terms, some may have needed further education in social skills; subjectively, all rejected any ideas of their personal social incompetence. As a result, it might be argued that, for them, the provision of all 'social' training 'on the job' was not only relatively effective (in that it was received), but also sufficient.

CONCLUSIONS

It should be clear that this paper has not attempted to talk generally about client responses to the Youth Opportunities Programme. Instead, it has focused on a particular category of male 16- to 19-year-old trainees which is significantly differentiated from official categorisations of YOP trainees and assumptions made about them. This category - or more precisely the two sub-groups for whom YOP is perceived as a constructive alternative to employment - hold perspectives about YOP which are quite distinct from official versions of the purposes and goals of YOP. Although there is little doubt that there is a 'hierarchy' of schemes which cater for young people with different levels of ability, this category of trainee would appear to be far larger than has been acknowledged (and a rapidly increasing proportion as the number of 'real' jobs for young people decline, thus propelling more and more 'normal' young people into YOP), with concomitant implications for the operation of the programme.

A central dilemma for YOP lies in its attempt to combine the twin objectives of training, education and work. Certainly, for the two groups of trainees referred to in this study, a unanimous preference was expressed for just work and there was pervasive dislike of the non-work aspects of YOP, such as 'social and life skills', whether it was offered off the job (at a college) or 'on the job' (but still in a formal manner). Similar topics discussed informally on the job, however, were not interpreted as such.

These trainees also developed far greater rapport with 'working-class' supervisors than with their 'professional' counterparts. The reasons for this have been explained. Yet in the light of the current employment situation and the receding job prospects for not only YOP clients but also other young unskilled people, it may in fact be the 'social and life skills' element of YOP which is more important in terms of informing these young people about the problems and realities of unemployment (while attempting to avoid the morally questionable role of 'adjusting' them to imminent unemployment). Whether or not the education and training element of YOP as it is currently offered in an increasingly institutionalised and the professionalised form is the most appropriate style of presentation remains debatable.

NOTES

1 I would like to express my thanks to Gill Coffin for her helpful
comments, to my colleagues in Oxford with whom the broader research on the Youth Opportunities Programme is being undertaken
and to the MSC who funded some of the research work upon which
this chapter draws.

Chapter 9

SOCIAL AND LIFE SKILLS: THE LATEST CASE OF COMPENSATORY EDUCATION

Paul Atkinson, Teresa L. Rees, David Shone and Howard Williamson

INTRODUCTION: THE DEMORALISED ADOLESCENT

The prospect of mass youth unemployment is widely regarded not only as a symptom of economic decline; it is also seen as a threat of moral decline. As Mungham shows elsewhere in this volume (chapter 3), unemployed youth give rise to 'moral panics', and are commonly portrayed by politicians and the mass media as a potential threat to the social fabric. This has given rise to fears of dangerous consequences, which go far beyond the immediate industrial and economic effects. Some have claimed to find evidence for the most alarming conclusions, and have seen fit to warn the public, educators and politicians accordingly. As Mungham shows, the overwhelming absence of social disorder has done nothing to assuage these misgivings.

The most extreme effects of unemployment are predicted to be the drift of young people into crime, violence and political extremism. These are held to be the likely outcome of 'disaffection', 'estrangement' and 'boredom' on the part of young people. The British Youth Council, for instance, has given us the following portrait of the demoralised adolescent:

> To be unemployed is to be excluded and this inevitably conditions how a person perceives the social structure and his or her position in it - at the bottom of the pile. Whether cynicism and antagonism or resignation and passivity take over a young person, the chances are that he or she will not easily take or use opportunities when they do arise to re-embark on a steady and satisfying adult working life, thus sustaining a pattern of deprivation (BYC, 1977, para.1).

Whether or not the demoralised youngster turns to social disorder, then, he or she will be handicapped by such attitudes and self-perceptions. The solution which is proposed to counteract such deleterious effects, then, is the 'moral rearmament' of the young unemployed. The British Youth Council document continues to the effect that: 'Youngsters have to be equipped with the instincts and social skills to lift themselves out of their situation' (ibid., p.25).

Demoralisation is thus proposed as a result of youth unemployment, and this chapter is concerned with those interventions aimed
at instilling into the young people those 'social skills to lift
themselves out of their situation'. This indeed has become a
major component of state intervention, via the MSC and the Youth
Opportunities Programme. It has given rise, we shall argue, to a
massive exercise in 'compensatory education' - an exercise about
which we have grave reservations.

As Mungham also documents, the perceived need to fortify the
moral status of young people without work may be pressing, given
the dire prognostications which have been made. For instance, Mr
Stanley Dixon, the President of the National Association of Head-
teachers, declared that the unemployment figures (in 1976) were:

> tragic for the individual, shameful for our society, and poli-
> tically explosive. This vast army may not be as organised as
> the NUS, but I can assure you they are a far more fertile
> breeding ground for revolution than all the sociological de-
> partments of our universities rolled into one ('Guardian', 1
> June 1976, cited in Frith, 1978b).

In much the same vein, in the Welsh Grand Committee debate on
youth unemployment in Wales, one member declared that

> Another frightening possibility is that, through sheer bore-
> dom, many of our young people in Wales may be attracted to
> the National Front. We must remember that Hitler, whatever
> else he may have done, certainly put Germany back to work
> ('Hansard', 30 January 1978).

During that same debate Leo Abse drew attention to the case of
Italy - where, he suggested, there was a coalition between, on
the one hand, young graduates and the offspring of the rich, and,
on the other hand, the unemployed 'dispossessed proletarian'
youth. He concluded that 'The Red Brigade of Italy may be a pre-
monition of what could come to the whole of Europe.' Similarly,
Nicholas Edwards suggested that 'Quite apart from the social and
economic waste involved it is sowing the seeds of violence, unrest
and extremism in the future.'

This is held to be particularly likely among young people from
ethnic minority groups who are known to have disproportionately
high rates of youth unemployment. In the course of a House of
Commons debate Edward Heath linked youth unemployment and immigra-
tion in these terms, noting that in the past,

> a vast number of immigrants came in. Their children have had
> all the benefits of the British system of education, and they
> are asking for the same sort of jobs as those with whom they
> have been educated. They are being three times as disappointed,
> however. In those circumstances can one be surprised, with
> young people not able to get jobs on this scale, that there is
> an increase in street violence, an increase in mugging and an
> increase in juvenile delinquency? ('Hansard', 30 January 1978).

Hence the morally damaging effects of unemployment are often
coupled with the social conditions of ethnic minorities in Britain -
particularly young West Indians. Accounts of the riots in the St
Paul's area of Bristol in April 1980, for instance, placed emphasis
on the high rates of unemployment among young urban blacks:

Community leaders estimate that there are four times as many
young blacks out of work as whites, and that in St Paul's
perhaps 75% of young blacks are unemployed. Many have dropped
out of the system altogether, having played truant during their
last school years and not bothering to register for work....
Unemployment and hostility to the police were probably the two
main immediate causes of what happened ('Sunday Times', 4 May
1980).

Similarly,

Chief Inspector Derek Lane, community relations officer for
the Avon and Somerset police, blamed high unemployment and discrimination against black youth on the job market for the ex-
plosion. He estimated that in Bristol a black youth had to
make at least ten applications before being considered for a
job whereas a white youth made about four ('The Times', 5
April 1980).

Many commentators at the time of the St Paul's riots drew attention to the fact that the essential ingredients for such events
existed in many other areas:

That something so violent could be so easily triggered in an
area like St Paul's does not augur well. Against a background
of recession, thousands of black Britons will be leaving school
over the next few years doomed to fester in inner cities
('Sunday Times', 4 May 1981).

Some even predicted correctly a precise location for such future
rioting - in Brixton - observing that 'vacancies for all ages ad-
vertised at the Brixton job centre have gone down ... (it is) particularly bad for black school leavers' ('Sunday Times', 15 June
1980). It has also been suggested that unemployed young blacks
will turn to crime: 'Two out of ten black school leavers in
London are turning to crime because they cannot get a job'
('Guardian', 27 July 1979) and that there is a growing discontent
over race relations in the Cardiff area with regard to social conditions and job opportunities which could lead to street violence
('Western Mail', 16 October 1980).

One of the recurrent ways in which youth unemployment is portrayed, then, as a 'moral panic', is in terms of its damaging
effects upon the moral fibre of young people. At the same time
such moral failure may also be put forward as a prime cause of
their inability to find work.

Such feelings may emerge from another of those contemporary
fears - that work has lost its meaning, and that the values and
attitudes associated with work have been undermined. Jahoda arti-
culates this feeling:

The most relevant of these value changes is the demise of the
protestant work ethic. The idea that work will bring salvation
in the hereafter, has all but disappeared with increasing secu-
larisation.

But the secular interpretation of the protestant work ethic
(if this is not a contradiction in terms) maintains that work is
meaningful beyond providing one's living, and that the unemployed would suffer from the absence of this additional meaning,
even if they did not suffer in their standard of living. If

this meaning has disappeared, as is often asserted, the experience of loss of work may have changed in a radical fashion
(1979).

Among young people seeking entry to the labour market such
supposed changing values may be translated crudely into the charge
that they are 'work shy', or in slightly more sophisticated terms,
that they are inappropriately socialised in some way. Such 'inappropriate' socialisation is not held to determine only the young
people's attitudes and values, of course. As Finn points out elsewhere in this volume (chapter 4), the 'debate' concerning industry
and schooling has been addressed both to issues of specific vocational skills and training, and also to the conditions for the renewal of an appropriately socialised work-force. This view has
been echoed by Reader, who suggests that

> The 'needs' of industry have not only, or even mainly, been
> expressed in terms of cognitive requirements, and the interest
> in pre-employment courses derives also from the more tradi-
> tional concerns of some employers in the social experiences and
> welfare of youth, a concern which, in the past, has combined a
> sense of social responsibility with anxieties about the loyal-
> ties and docility of the workforce (1979, p.140).

Popular images of the contemporary adolescent seeking (or perhaps not even seeking) employment are couched in terms of a lack of
basic competences such as literacy and numeracy, and - in the most
general sense - a certain 'moral' deficiency. Thus the young person is seen as poorly or unrealistically motivated, as inept at
handling social relationships with clients, customers and colleagues,
and as improperly prepared to meet the demands of the world of work.

It comes as no surprise, therefore, that Manpower Services
Commission (MSC) programmes - particularly the Youth Opportunities
Programme (YOP) - are designed to inculcate the (supposedly) appropriate knowledge, experience, attitudes and values in preparing
young people for employment. Such socialisation explicitly con-
tains elements which are designed to enhance the 'moral' status of
poorly qualified school-leavers. This so-called 'Social and Life
Skills' (SLS) component is a direct response to the views outlined
above, on the twin aspects of unemployment as cause and effect of
demoralisation. These policies which have been implemented by the
MSC have implicitly relied upon a form of 'compensatory education',
aimed at reproducing appropriately socialised young workers who are
ready for participation in the labour market, or who will form a
pool of labour power when (supposedly) the market expands once
more. By means of such intervention the youngsters will not simply
be protected from the worst effects of unemployment itself, but
their employability will be enhanced through their moral improvement.

Of course, the experience of 'work', through work-experience
schemes, work-introduction courses and the like, is viewed as
morally therapeutic in itself. Quite apart from current concerns
with mass long-term unemployment, there is a history of work being
endowed with powers for moral improvement. The equation of idleness,
sin and vice is fundamental to our ideologies of work, as in the corresponding equivalence of industry and virtue. Work has been var-
iously promoted as morally therapeutic in such settings as lunatic
asylums, workhouses, prison workshops, geriatric wards and so on.

Work thus provides intrinsic as well as extrinsic rewards. The
protestant ethic is, par excellence, the celebration of the moral
worth and purpose of work.

Over and above the experience of work itself, contemporary intervention by MSC explicitly provides for moral enhancement,
through the teaching of 'Social and Life Skills'. Not only does
this cope with the fears of demoralisation as effect of unemployment, it is also designed to tackle such deficiencies as cause of
'failure' in the labour market.

SOCIAL AND LIFE SKILLS

The rationale for SLS is outlined in the Foreword to the MSC
'Instructional Guide': 'Training means more than the acquisition
of specific skills to perform certain tasks. It also involves an
understanding of the wider social aspects of working life' (MSC,
1976c). The Guide goes on to suggest that 'Many people lack some
of the basic skills which most of us take for granted' (ibid., p.1).
The SLS course, then, is designed to encourage the development of
such competencies in the unemployed youngster.

The 'skills' referred to are described as 'all those abilities,
bits of information, know how, and decision making which we need to
get by in life.' Two areas are identified: 'social skills' are
those which are primarily involved in the conduct of interpersonal
relations; 'life skills' are those which are more involved in the
planning and management of daily activities. (The MSC guidelines
themselves acknowledge that there is a degree of overlap implied
in this distinction.)

Social skills in the workplace are said to involve aspects of
'communication', 'behaviour', 'appearance' and 'attitude', along
with the attributes of 'mixing in' and 'taking orders'. In private life they contribute to 'making friends', 'conversation' and
'resisting provocation'. Life skills are specified as those involved in 'getting information or advice, handling money, familiarity with essential services etc.', or 'coping skills'. They
also comprise job-finding abilities, such as looking, choosing,
applying for and securing employment, as well as leisure activities - 'hobbies', 'interests' and 'clubs'.

The general objective of SLS training is the inculcation of a
large number of diverse and vaguely defined skills to unemployed
adolescents, in order to improve not only their chances of finding
a job, but also their ability to hold down a job when they find
one. The 'Instructional Guide' provides advice to tutors con-
ducting such courses (which are provided in colleges of further
education, and in the workplace). As well as providing guidelines
as to course content it also suggests how best to achieve specific
objectives.

The proposed methods of instruction include: group discussion,
counselling, and role playing. Group discussion is given considerable emphasis as a means of modifying negative attitudes to work,
to counteract 'alienation from work', and enhance 'timekeeping and
attendance', 'quality of work' and 'job satisfaction'. It is clear
that the preferred approach is what is referred to as a 'patterned'

discussion: tutors should initiate discussions with controversial
questions while allowing time for participation from the students
and providing summaries at strategic points.

Counselling is regarded as suitable for attitude reformation on
an individual basis, together with the monitoring of work-related
progress, or regress. This is also said to be of value in determining that the potentials and interests of particular trainees are
suited to the job applications they make.

A great deal of stress is placed on skills related to job finding. A large proportion of suggested course content is devoted to
exercises such as the writing of letters and completion of application forms, and role playing involving the rehearsal of job interviews.

Remaining objectives which are stated in the 'Instructional
Guide' include the following: 'to develop ability to communicate';
'to develop ability to cope with adult life'; 'to develop knowledge of local facilities'; 'to develop the ability to cope with
calculations associated with various jobs'; 'to develop job seeking ability'; 'to develop ability to retain employment'.

According to the Guide, coping with adult life may include such
practical issues as the knowledge relevant to wiring an electric
fuse or plug, or changing a tap washer. The development of
trainees' knowledge of local facilities may involve a discussion of
how to take up and be involved in such activities as 'ballroom
dancing' or 'model making'.

It will be apparent that the projected content of SLS training
varies from the very specific to the most general. They add up to
a most diverse package. Overall, however, their rationale is quite
clear. The aims embodied in the 'Instructional Guide' are, in educational terms, very familiar - a programme of 'compensatory education'. Social and Life Skills provision is designed to instil
in young people cultural and cognitive resources which they are
thought to have missed out on (for reasons unspecified). For
these unemployed adolescents SLS courses function like the 'finish-
ing school' for more fortunate youngsters who are 'coming out'.
They furnish the necessary social graces.

Such an approach implies, in part at least, that the young unemployed are disadvantaged in seeking employment because they are
deficient in relevant and acceptable abilities, experience, moti-
vations and attitudes. Specific skills which are central to the
MSC special programmes - such as numeracy - are thus paralleled
and complemented by the more diffuse features of social and communicative competence.

A CASE OF COMPENSATORY EDUCATION

As such SLS courses have a good deal in common with previous
attempts to identify and remedy cultural 'deficits'. The majority
of such interventions have been aimed at the pre-school and early
school years. They flourished during the 1960s on both sides of
the Atlantic. They too were predicated on the belief that manifest
inequalities in educational attainment could be rectified by various
forms of positive discrimination in favour of the 'disadvantaged'.

Such policies were often informed by crude versions of 'linguistic deficit', based on vulgar misrepresentations of the sociolinguistic theories of Bernstein. (For a thorough review of linguistic deficit theories, including an exposition and critique of Bernstein, see Dittmar, 1976.) Hence compensatory initiatives were frequently aimed at improving linguistic skills, as well as numeracy and similar cognitive abilities.

The earlier attempts at cultural compensation have been subject to stringent criticism, and similar reservations can be voiced in the context of SLS provision. At root, such intervention seems to rest on a very shaky understanding of culture and communicative competence. There is no justification for regarding 'disadvantaged' groups - be they urban black Americans or British working-class adolescents - as lacking in culture, in seeing their existing resources as unformed, inadequate or missing altogether. They may be inappropriate for certain purposes in some social contexts, but that is a very different matter: we shall return to it below.

Commentators on compensatory education have pointed out that the very idea of 'cultural deprivation' is, strictly speaking, incoherent since the target populations are in no sense 'deprived' of their own culture. On the contrary they can be viewed as highly proficient in it, provided that such cultures be approached in their own terms, rather than simply being evaluated in a negative fashion (see, for example, Keddie, 1973, Introduction). The work of Labov on the logical and expressive possibilities of Black English Vernacular is an important reference point in this regard, providing as it does strong evidence against the notion of linguistic deficit (Labov, 1972).

There is clearly a danger that SLS training merely recapitulates such basic misapprehensions as underpinned the compensatory schemes of a decade or so earlier. The 'Instructional Guide' touches on supposed deficiencies among young people, and lists some of the 'skills' which they may be presumed to lack. There is no sense here of what cultural competence the young people themselves might actually possess. While the surface tone of the guidelines is positive and encouraging, the underlying message is profoundly negative in its image of unemployed adolescents.

The image is dominated by an implicit model of a sort of cultural vacuum which can be filled by the provision of suitable remedial treatment. This rests on an extremely crude view of social life and socialisation. This is a criticism which can be levelled at most forms of compensatory education, but it is particularly pertinent in the case of young school-leavers. By the time they have reached adolescence such young men and women are highly socialised. They are not incompetent and socially unformed (though there will be aspects of adult life with which they are unfamiliar). They are highly developed and proficient social beings.

In comparing SLS courses and earlier attempts at compensatory education, it is worth noting that both tend to operate at the margins of formal, compulsory education. While former schemes were aimed largely at children of pre-school and early school age, SLS caters for school-leavers who have not yet entered long-term employment. Both therefore operate at transitional phases into and out of full-time schooling. In passing, it is also worth noting that some of the recipients of YOP in the 1970s may, as infants, have been the beneficiaries of compensatory education in the 1960s.

SLS therefore, like its pre-school predecessors in the field of compensatory education, is open to further criticism. As Bernstein has vigorously maintained, compensatory education served to deflect potential scrutiny and criticism away from the education system itself. Bernstein argued (1971) that the notion of 'compensatory education' was hardly appropriate when the relevant populations had not been offered an adequate educational environment in the first place. In a similar way we can see that SLS and the like also focus attention on the presumed failures and shortcomings of unemployed adolescents themselves. While the MSC document 'Making Experience Work' states that YOP 'aims to make all young people employable, and does not stigmatise a particular group as being unemployable' (MSC, 1978b), nevertheless the identification of some young people as, apparently, culturally deficient or incompetent is hardly compatible with such a high flown and impartial ideal.

SLS and similar provisions are not only marginal to the educational system: they mediate between school and work. And the remarks made about schooling apply to industrial life as well. Failure to enter or to maintain a position in the world of work is likewise all too easily attributed to the perceived inadequacies of unemployed school leavers. It has been remarked in the context of the so-called 'Great Debate' on education generally that the 'needs' of industry - as formulated by its spokespersons and political allies - are all too often treated unquestioningly as a basis for criticising schools and their products. This is apparent for SLS - where problems of work and industry are all too easily conceived of in terms of a 'deficit' model, where explanation of 'failure' is couched in terms of individual pathology, and where the diagnosis of deficiencies rests on unexamined value judgments.

Overall, then, SLS and similar forms of intervention suffer common limitations at a conceptual level. They remain marginal to the major institutions which they are designed to affect. They give the appearance of amelioration without actual change in the conditions which give rise to the underlying problems. They embody the classic approach to social 'pathology' - a tendency to blame the victim.

PRACTICAL PROBLEMS

There must be reservations about the practical efficacy - indeed the feasibility - of SLS training. It is far from clear whose version of social life should be endorsed in such courses - those of college teachers, employers, or the youngsters themselves. There is a consensus that such training should relate to work - but whose definition and experience of work is it to be, the CBI, the TUC, local employers, the careers service, young unskilled workers? Is the teacher to take as the frame of reference the workplace, or the young people's own life and experience? Robins and Cohen, writing in a more general context suggest that any educational process for such adolescents should be 'rooted in the peer group uses

of language and literacy, as well as the oral traditions through
which the residual forms of working class knowledge are trans-
mitted' (Robins and Cohen, 1978, p.176). Although it is unwise to
overemphasise the contrast between working-class 'oral' culture,
and a 'literate' culture of the school or college, Robins and Cohen
are right to suggest that education which takes no account of working-class youth culture will not reap many rewards.

Almost by definition, in fact, the sort of teenagers for whom
YOP was designed will be just those who have not done well with
formal educational provision. As a relevant MSC document has
pointed out

It is young people of lower ability, or few development opportunities, who are most at risk. It is just this highly disparate group whom school has often failed, who have not been
students in colleges of further education in the past and whose
industrial or work training has been most rudimentary, if it
has existed at all. As a generality, the education services
and the trainers (both private and public) have little experience of successfully providing learning experiences for the
acquisition of the skills which these young people need:
manual skills, mathematical and communication skills, interpersonal and social skills and the ability and confidence to
face uncertain and complex situations (MSC, nd).

As we have suggested, the point about what such young people
may 'need' is debatable, but the general observation concerning
educators is a valid one. They certainly have little relevant
experience. The substance of the literature on youth culture,
education and the transition from school to work amply demonstrates
the failure of traditional educational measures for this category
of young people. It also points to their rejection of such provision, and of the teachers involved.

Nevertheless, there has been a fervent attempt to incorporate
a specifically educational element into provision for the young
unemployed, which includes, as well as SLS, the aims of enhancing
motivation, teaching basic job skills, providing personal and
careers counselling and continuing general education. But there
are few, if any, grounds for believing that continuing education
will succeed where the initial education apparently failed.

In any case it is hard to see how an adequate training in 'Social
and Life Skills' could actually be provided. When one looks beyond
the vague generalities of the 'Instructional Guide' it becomes apparent that the issues are extremely complex - so complex as almost
to defy analysis. We know precious little about the nature of
'Social and Life Skills' - about, that is, the awesomely detailed
and subtle ways in which we organise our everyday social interaction. We are still at the stage of scraping the surface. The
work of ethnomethodologists, some linguists and others has begun
to explicate the minutiae of everyday life. But as yet our knowledge is rudimentary.

By its very nature, the sort of social competence dealt with by
SLS is unselfconscious. As the MSC's own guide points out, they
are 'skills which most of us take for granted.' We are not normally aware of our own language and gestures. Although Goffman
(1971) may invite such a reading, our 'self presentation' is not

normally a matter for careful and self-conscious manipulation.
Those times when we are forced to confront them in everyday life
are usually occasions of embarrassment, of some failure in communication. Self-consciousness does not come easily to any of us,
and certainly does not come easily to most adolescents.

Thus it is all but impossible for 'teachers' of SLS themselves
to analyse and adapt systematically such social behaviour. Even
'specialist' teachers in the colleges will rarely have the basic
analytic skills. By the same token it will be extremely hard for
young adults to confront and adapt their everyday social activities.
Teachers and students alike, then, are likely to find themselves
working in a vacuum, lacking a shared public language in which to
formulate the tasks they are supposed to engage in.

We are not suggesting that social life and skills are inherently
incapable of description. Rather, as we have suggested, they demand a highly developed technical expertise. Attempts to deal with
them on a commonsense basis are almost guaranteed to be severely
limited. Reference to the MSC's SLS 'Instructional Guide' shows
just how blunt a weapon it is. Many of the 'Social and Life Skills'
are vague in the extreme. It is far removed from any systematic,
principled analysis of everyday life. It is not our criticism that
the MSC has failed to produce a scholarly analysis of social interaction; rather that in the absence of any systematic body of knowledge there can be no adequate curriculum or pedagogy. Teachers
can be forgiven if they fall back on such 'traditional', formal
educational practices as drilling students in writing job application letters (which could well have some immediate benefit, but
hardly matches up to the more grandiose claims of SLS).

Thus far we have been considering SLS as an ideal and have suggested that in its very conception it is problematic. However, we
should now like to move onto a rather different sort of analysis,
that is, of the actual working of SLS. Then problems and issues
of a wholly different kind are raised.

The main difficulty in examining these in practice is that remarkably little empirical evaluation has been carried out. While
some considerable work is being undertaken on SLS at the defini-
tional and conceptual level by the National Foundation for Education Research (NFER), for example, examinations of what actually
happens appears to be confined to a sample survey of YOP participants conducted by MSC. This showed that 23 per cent of a sample
of 2,780 young people on YOP were receiving some form of 'off the
job' training or education, but not all of this would necessarily
be SLS. The MSC survey underlines the difficulty in securing
reliable estimates of how much (let alone what kind) of SLS is
actually taught; this is caused partly by the dilemma of whether
to count people or places given the complications of high turnover
and high rates of absenteeism, not to mention what have been described - somewhat obscurely - as 'computing difficulties'.

Our own work in this area is rather limited but, we hope, illustrative. In the first instance in order to assess how much SLS
is being taught in the four counties of industrial South Wales we
contacted all the appropriate colleges. From the information given
to us we calculated that only one-third of the colleges were involved in teaching SLS on YOP and that only 10 per cent of YOP

participants were receiving SLS in colleges (although there are a few other venues). This figure was accepted by officials in the Office for Manpower Services Commission in Wales as being in line with their estimate for Wales as a whole.

Our inquiries suggested that courses in South Wales varied enormously in terms of level of staffing and resources, course content and 'benefit' accruing to the YOP participants. It was clear that on the whole SLS was 'low status' and in some colleges resource allocation was minimal, SLS taking second place to the more lucrative (for the college) MSC Training Opportunities Scheme (TOPS) courses.

Contrasting two specific SLS courses in South Wales, one in a college and one 'on the job', enables us to illustrate some of the points made earlier in this paper about SLS as compensatory education. It also serves to demonstrate the wide interpretation made of the concept of SLS in the face of more pragmatic issues, rendering some of NFER's agonising rather redundant.

In the college course we examined, a business studies lecturer had responsibility for SLS added to his teaching load with four days notice. The syllabus was designed, almost on a week-by-week basis, with far more consideration of who was free to teach, when and where rather than what should be taught. As a result, while some attention was paid to teaching the young people about how to look for a job and how to behave at interviews, considerably more time was spent on health education and communication, as the staff specialising in those areas were available to teach on the appropriate day. If SLS had happened to be arranged for another day of the week, the syllabus would have looked quite different.

The participants were all girls with about five O-levels each; they were on the whole well motivated with, perhaps because of their age, almost meticulous self-presentation. This raised questions about their recruitment to SLS as it seemed unlikely that of all the YOP participants in this youth unemployment blackspot these girls were most 'in need of SLS'. It transpired that the principle underlying recruitment to the course was to ease the administrative burden of obtaining employers' consent by only contacting those employers with a sizeable number of young people on YOP. Inevitably these tended to be local authorities offering clerical work experience to qualified girls.

By contrast the participants at the second SLS course we studied were all boys with no qualifications at all. Half of them had been in some sort of trouble with the police. Attending the on the job SLS course was an integral part of the activities of the placement on YOP at this community centre. Rather than being taught by college lecturers, the staff on this course included a community tutor, a probation student and an adult literacy tutor. A substantial amount of time and thought was given to the preparation of the course including visits to courses at other centres. The workplace was able to provide duplicating and video equipment, a minibus, two comfortable rooms and other back-up resources. The staff had a good network of outside contacts which meant, for example, that programmes of factory visits could be arranged.

The participants were clearly competent in the lifestyle of their neighbourhood but were being taught how to abandon that in order

to conform to the norms of wider society. So, for example, when
during a video-taped mock interview one youth explained he had
gained his experience in plastering on 'fiddles' with his father,
it was explained that this was not appropriate information to bring
up in a job interview. To which another youth pointed out that the
instructors did not really understand how people 'like them' got
jobs: 'I'd never actually go for an interview. I'm only interested
in the labouring and I'd just go down a site and ask.' Most of the
youths felt SLS was just a 'skive off work'.

Clearly we would not suggest that these examples of how SLS is
taught, and to whom, are any more than examples and considerably
more work is required. However, they do serve to illustrate some
of the operational difficulties involved in teaching SLS.

SUBVERSIVE SKILLS

The fact that 'Social and Life Skills' are not well understood does
not detract from the fact that in the worlds of work and education
people may be stigmatised and suffer by virtue of essentially tri-
vial cultural reasons. Accent and dialect, dress and demeanour
may be evaluated negatively by those who have the power to impose
such evaluations (teachers, careers officers, potential employers
and so on). One does not need to subscribe to a very strong version of 'labelling' theory in order to recognise that such gate-
keepers' judgments may have real consequences for young people
whom they judge adversely.

Conceivably, then, there might be some merit in teaching some
version of SLS as a 'subversive' activity (if we granted that a
limited exercise in social and life skills would be feasible).
Willis (1977) has suggested that working-class adolescents (or at
least, his 'lads') may be capable of 'penetrations' of education
and labour. In simple terms, they can 'see through' social institutions – although such penetrations are not wholly articulated, or
consciously and explicitly formulated. Rather than lacking an
appreciation of the world of work, they may indeed have a lively –
and from their point of view realistic – understanding of it.

From this point of view SLS might be mobilised to help young
men and women to manipulate social events to their own advantage,
rather than an attempt to mould the youngsters for their own good.
They would thus be equipped with the communicative resources for
'strategic interaction' (see Goffman, 1969). Such an approach
would recognise explicitly the young people's existing resources
and understandings, rather than assuming that their stock of knowledge is simply inadequate or missing. This perspective would
match the realism, even cynicism, that many adolescents express.
While such 'subversive' work might find little favour in official
quarters, it could well prove more realistic in the long run. It
would recognise too that while young people are not in any meaningful sense 'culturally deprived', they may be 'deprived' none the
less by virtue of arbitrary cultural reasons.

We are sceptical of attempts to remedy the supposed deficiencies
of working-class adolescents. That does not mean that we deny the
value of providing them with extra cultural resources. There is a

difference between the two positions. The latter recognises the adolescents themselves as competent, adequately socialised members of a culture and recognises too their potential ability to 'penetrate' the institutions they encounter.

In conclusion it should be pointed out that through the expansion of MSC programmes there is a considerable expansion of education and training, often located in colleges of further education, which in effect has bypassed the education sector. This has led to some difficulties and tension at the organisational level, but more fundamentally the overall ethos of the new element which has been introduced is suspect. As Locke and Pratt have recently pointed out,

> The education service has been watching the progress of the MSC with some rivalry and even acrimony. Courses promoted by the TSA through TOPS had benefited colleges, but further education teachers were not as a body happy with the narrowness of the training (1979, p.47).

There is a fear that what is being promoted is a philistine, anti-intellectual climate, in which education is regarded solely from the point of view of producing an appropriately socialised workforce.

We have argued that the contribution of Social and Life Skills courses in the Youth Opportunities Programme is a form of 'compensatory education' aimed at the production of more amenable employees. Like other compensatory programmes before it, it is based on an inadequate view of the culture of the target population. Like them it deflects potential criticism away from educational and industrial provision as such. It confirms unemployed teenagers as 'failures', and translates their lack of work into a personal failure. It represents the structural problems of youth unemployment in terms of the individual characteristics of unemployed youths.

NOTES

1 This chapter is based on preliminary, unfunded research on Social and Life Skills training undertaken by the authors in the Sociological Research Unit, Department of Sociology, University College, Cardiff.

BIBLIOGRAPHY

ARCHER, T. (1865), 'The Pauper, The Thief and The Convict', London: Groombridge.

BARKER, R. (1972), 'Education and Politics, 1900-51: A Study of the Labour Party', London: Oxford University Press.

BARKER, J. and DOWNING, H. (1980), Word processing and the transformation of the patriarchal relations of control in the office, 'Capital and Class', no. 10, pp.64-9.

BEN-DAVID, J. (1963-4), Professions in the class systems of present day societies, 'Current Sociology', 12 (3), pp.256-61.

BERNSTEIN, B. (1971), Education cannot compensate for society, ch. 10 in 'Class, Codes and Control', vol. 1, London: Paladin.

BLACKBURN, R. and MANN, M. (1979), 'The Working Class in the Labour Market', London: Macmillan.

BOARD OF EDUCATION (1924), Report of the Juvenile Organizations Committee of the Board of Education on the problem of the unemployed juvenile between 14 and 16 years of age, PRO, Cab.27/267.

BOARD OF TRADE (1932), 'An industrial survey of South Wales' (made by the University College of South Wales and Monmouthshire), London: HMSO.

BRANSON, N. and HEINEMANN, M. (1971), 'Britain in the Nineteen Thirties', London: Weidenfeld & Nicolson.

BRITISH YOUTH COUNCIL (1977), 'Youth Unemployment: Causes and Cures', London: BYC.

CENTRAL ADVISORY COUNCIL FOR EDUCATION (ENGLAND) (1963), 'Half Our Future' (Newsom Report), London: HMSO.

CENTRAL POLICY REVIEW STAFF (1980), 'Education, Training and Industrial Performance', London: HMSO.

CENTRE FOR CONTEMPORARY CULTURAL STUDIES EDUCATION GROUP (1981), 'Unpopular Education: Schooling and Social Democracy Since 1944', London: Hutchinson.

CHESNEY, K. (1970), 'The Victorian Underworld', London: Temple Smith.

COMMITTEE ON WELSH AFFAIRS (1980), 'The Role of the Welsh Office and Associated Bodies in Developing Employment Opportunities in Wales', vol.1, London: HMSO.

CORRIGAN, P. (1979), 'Schooling the Smash Street Kids', London: Macmillan.

128

CORRIGAN, P. and CORRIGAN, P. (1977), Labour and the State (mimeo), paper presented to the BSA annual conference.

COX, C.B. and DYSON, A.E. (1969a), 'Fight for education: a black paper', Critical Quarterly Society.

COX, C.B. and DYSON, A.E. (1969b), 'Black paper II: crisis in education', Critical Quarterly Society.

COX, C.B. and DYSON, A.E. (1970). 'Black paper III: goodbye Mr. Short', Critical Quarterly Society.

COUNTY BOROUGH OF NEWPORT (1933), Chief Constable's annual report for the year ended 1933.

DALY, M. (1938), The social consequences of industrial transference: a reply, 'Sociological Review', 30 (3), pp.236-61.

DANIEL, G. (1940), Some factors affecting the movement of labour, 'Oxford Economic Papers', 3, pp.144-79.

DEPARTMENT OF EDUCATION AND SCIENCE (1976), 'Unified Vocational Preparation: A Pilot Approach: A Government Statement', London: HMSO.

DEPARTMENT OF EDUCATION AND SCIENCE (1977), 'Education in Schools: A Consultative Document', London: HMSO.

DEPARTMENT OF EDUCATION AND SCIENCE (1979), '16 to 18: Education and Training for 16-18 year olds: A Consultative Paper', London: HMSO.

DEPARTMENT OF EMPLOYMENT (1977), MSC evaluates job creation, DE 'Gazette', 85, 3, March 1977, pp.211-17.

DEPARTMENT OF EMPLOYMENT (1978), 'Employment News', March 1978.

DEPARTMENT OF EMPLOYMENT (1980), First-off-16 year olds entering employment in 1978, 'Employment Gazette', vol.88, no.12, pp.1201-3.

DEVON, J. (1912), 'The Criminal and the Community', London: John Lane.

DITTMAR, N. (1976), 'Sociolinguistics', London: Edward Arnold.

'ECONOMIST' (1977), Youth on the dole, 'Economist', 11 June, pp. 87-90.

FINN, D. and FRITH, S. (1980), Education and the labour market, Open University course unit (E353), Open University Press.

FRITH, S. (1978a), Education, training and the labour process (mimeo), paper presented to the conference of Socialist Economists Education Group.

FRITH, S. (1978b), 'The Sociology of Rock', London: Constable.

FRYER, J. (1977), Who wants to work in a factory?, 'Sunday Times', 20 November.

FURTHER EDUCATION CURRICULUM REVIEW AND DEVELOPMENT UNIT (1978), 'Survey Report of FE Provision for Young Unemployed 1977', London: DES.

GARSIDE, W.R. (1976), Juvenile unemployment statistics between the wars: a commentary and guide to sources, 'Bulletin of the Society for the Study of Labour History', 33, pp.38-46.

GARSIDE, W.R. (1977), Juvenile unemployment and public policy between the wars, 'Economic History Review', 2nd series, 30 (2), pp.322-39.

GERSHUNY, J.I. and PAHL, R.E. (1980), Britain in the decade of the three economies, 'New Society', vol.51, no.900, pp.7-9.

GILLIS, J.R. (1974), 'Youth and History', London: Academic Press.

GLEESON, D. and MARDLE, G. (1980), 'Further Education or Training: A Case Study in the Theory and Practice of Day Release Education', London: Routledge and Kegan Paul.

GOLLAN, J. (1936), 'Youth in British Industry', London: Gollanz.
GOFFMAN, E. (1969), 'Strategic Interaction', Oxford: Blackwell.
GOFFMAN, E. (1971), 'The Presentation of Self in Everyday Life',
Harmondsworth: Penguin.
GREGORY, D. and EDGAR, C. (1980), 'Youth unemployment and MSC spe-
cial programmes: Trade Union responses from Wales and the North
West of England', report prepared for MSC, Manchester: William
Temple Foundation.
GREGORY, D., MANNING, A., ATHERTON, J. and MARKALL, G. (1979),
'Youth employment - an action research programme', report prepared
for the Commission of the European Communities, Manchester: Wil-
liam Temple Foundation.
HALL, S. (1979), The great moving right show, 'Marxism Today',
January 1979.
HART, A.P. (1980), The black and white, 'New Universities Quar-
terly', 34 (4), pp.401-6.
HOBSBAWM, E. and RUDE, G. (1969), 'Captain Swing', London: Allen
Lane.
HOUSE OF COMMONS PUBLIC EXPENDITURE COMMITTEE (1976), 'Policy
Making in the Department of Education and Science', 10th report,
session 1975-6, London: HMSO.
HUSTON, L. (1972), The flowers of power: a critique of OFY and
LIP programmes, 'Our Generation', vol.8, no.4, pp.52-61.
JAHODA, M. (1979), The psychological meanings of unemployment,
'New Society', 6 September, pp.492-5.
JENNINGS, H. (1934), 'Brynmawr: A Study of a Distressed Area',
London: Allenson.
JESSOP, B. (1980), The transformation of the state in postwar
Britain, in R. Scase (ed.), 'The State in Western Europe', London:
Croom Helm.
JEWKES, J. and JEWKES, S. (1938), 'The Juvenile Labour Market',
London: Gollanz.
JEWKES, J. and WINTERBOTTOM, A. (1933), 'Juvenile Unemployment',
London: Allen & Unwin.
KEDDIE, N. (1973), 'Tinker, Tailor: The Myth of Cultural Depriva-
tion', Harmondsworth: Penguin.
LABOV, W. (1972), 'Language in the Inner City: Studies in the Black
English Vernacular', Philadelphia: University of Pennsylvania
Press.
LEAT, D. (1975), The rise and role of the poor man's lawyer',
'British Journal of Law and Society', 2 (2), pp.166-81.
LETCHWORTH, W.P. (1977), 'Report on Deprived and Delinquent
Children', London.
LEWIS COMMITTEE (1917), 'Departmental committee on juvenile educa-
tion in relation to employment after the war', final report, Cd.,
8512.
LOCKE, M. and PRATT, J. (1979), 'A Guide to Learning After School',
Harmondsworth: Penguin.
LUSH, A.J. (1941), 'The Young Adult in South Wales', Cardiff: Uni-
versity of Wales Press Board.
McCOSH, J. (1867), On compulsory education, 'Transactions of the
National Association for the promotion of social science'.
MAKEHAM, P. (1980), Youth unemployment: an examination of evidence
on youth unemployment using national statistics, 'Research Paper

No.10', London: Department of Employment.

MANPOWER RESEARCH GROUP (1980), Occupational change in the British economy, 'Employment Gazette', vol.88, no.12, pp.1204-8.

MANPOWER SERVICES COMMISSION (1976a), 'Annual Report 1975-6', London: MSC.

MANPOWER SERVICES COMMISSION (1976b), 'Towards a Comprehensive Manpower Policy', London: MSC.

MANPOWER SERVICES COMMISSION (1976c), 'Instructional Guide to Social and Life Skills', London: MSC.

MANPOWER SERVICES COMMISSION (1977a), 'Young People and Work', The Holland Report, London: MSC.

MANPOWER SERVICES COMMISSION (1977b), 'Review and Plan', London: MSC.

MANPOWER SERVICES COMMISSION (1978a), 'Review and Plan', London: MSC.

MANPOWER SERVICES COMMISSION (1978b), 'Making Experience Work: Principles and Guidelines for Providing Work Experience', London: MSC.

MANPOWER SERVICES COMMISSION (1979a), 'Review of the First Year of Special Programmes', London: MSC.

MANPOWER SERVICES COMMISSION (1979b), 'Notes on the conduct of STEP from December 1979' (internal document), London: MSC.

MANPOWER SERVICES COMMISSION (1980a), 'Review of the Second Year of Special Programmes', London: MSC.

MANPOWER SERVICES COMMISSION (1980b), 'Manpower Review 1980', London: MSC.

MANPOWER SERVICES COMMISSION (1980c), 'Outlook on Training: Review of the Employment and Training Act 1973', London: MSC.

MANPOWER SERVICES COMMISSION (1981a), 'Corporate Plan 1981-5', London: MSC.

MANPOWER SERVICES COMMISSION (1981b), 'Review of Services for the Unemployed', London MSC.

MANPOWER SERVICES COMMISSION (1981c), 'Manpower Review 1981', London MSC.

MANPOWER SERVICES COMMISSION (1981d), 'A New Training Initiative: a consultative document', London: MSC.

MANPOWER SERVICES COMMISSION (nd), 'Training for Skills: A Programme for Action', London: MSC.

MANPOWER SERVICES COMMISSION TRAINING SERVICES AGENCY (1975), 'Vocational Preparation for Young People', London: MSC:TSA.

MARQUAND, H. (1936), 'South Wales Needs a Plan', London: Allen & Unwin.

MEARA, G. (1936), 'Juvenile Unemployment in South Wales', Cardiff: University of Wales Press.

MIDDLEMAS, K. (1979), 'Politics in Industrial Society: The Experience of the British System Since 1911', London: Deutsch.

MILES, R. and PHIZACKLEA, A. (eds) (1978), 'Racism and Political Action in Britain', London: Routledge & Kegan Paul.

MINISTER OF LABOUR (1934), Memorandum on the establishment and conduct of courses of instruction for unemployed boys and girls (England and Wales), London: HMSO.

MINISTRY OF LABOUR (1929), Memorandum on the shortage, surplus and redistribution of juvenile labour during the years 1928 to 1933, based on the views of local juvenile employment committees, Cmnd. 3327.

MINISTRY OF LABOUR (1933), Report on juvenile unemployment for the
year 1933, London: Ministry of Labour.
MINISTRY OF LABOUR (1934a), Report on juvenile unemployment for the
year 1934, London: Ministry of Labour.
MINISTRY OF LABOUR (1934b), Reports of investigators into the in-
dustrial conditions in certain depressed areas: report on South
Wales and Monmouthshire, Cmnd. 4728.
MINISTRY OF LABOUR (1936), 'Ministry of Labour Gazette', 44 (7)
June.
MORGAN, A.E. (1939), 'The Needs of Youth: A Report Made to King
George's Jubilee Trust Fund', London: Oxford University Press.
MUKHERJEE, S. (1974), 'There's Work to be Done: Unemployment and
Manpower Policies', London: MSC/HMSO.
MUNGHAM, G. and PEARSON, G. (eds) (1976), 'Working Class Youth
Culture', London: Routledge & Kegan Paul.
NATIONAL ECONOMIC DEVELOPMENT OFFICE (1977), 'Engineering Crafts-
men: Shortages and Related Problems', London: HMSO.
NATIONAL INDUSTRIAL DEVELOPMENT COUNCIL OF WALES AND MONMOUTHSHIRE
(1937), 'The Second Industrial Survey of South Wales', vol.3,
Cardiff: University Press Board.
NATIONAL YOUTH EMPLOYMENT COUNCIL (1974), 'Unqualified, Untrained
and Unemployed', London: Department of Employment.
NEALE, W.B. (1840), 'Juvenile Delinquency in Manchester', Man-
chester.
O'BOYLE, L. (1970), The problem of an excess of educated men in
western Europe 1800-50, 'Journal of Modern History', vol.42, no.4,
pp.471-95.
O'BRIEN, R. Sir (1977), Josiah Mason Memorial Lecture, Birmingham.
OSBORN, W.C. (1860), 'The Preservation of Youth from Crime: A
Nation's Duty', London.
OWEN, A.D.K. (1937), The social consequences of industrial transference, 'Sociological Review', 34 (4) pp.331-54.
PAGE, A.C. (1977), State intervention in the inter-war period: the
special areas acts 1934-37, 'British Journal of Law and Society',
4, pp.175-203.
PARE, W. (1862), A plan for the suppression of the predatory
classes, London, 'Transactions of the Association for the Promo-
tion of Social Science'.
PEARSON, G. (1975), 'The Deviant Imagination', London: Macmillan.
PEARSON, G. (1976), 'Paki-Bashing' in a North-East Lancashire
cotton town, in G. Mungham and G. Pearson (eds) 'Working Class
Youth Culture', London: Routledge & Kegan Paul.
PHILLIPS, W. (1855), 'The Wild Tribes of London', London.
PIMLOTT, B. (1981), The North East: back to the 1930s, 'Political
Quarterly', 52 (1) pp.51-63.
PITFIELD, D.E. (1973), Labour migration and the regional problem in
Britain, 1920-1939, unpublished PhD thesis, University of Stirling.
PITFIELD, D.E. (1978), The quest for an effective regional policy,
1934-1937, 'Regional Studies', 12, pp.429-43.
POLLARD, S. (1962), 'The Development of the British Economy 1914-
1950', London: Edward Arnold.
POPE, R. (nd), 'Catering for the young unemployed: juvenile unem-
ployment centres in inter-war Britain', mimeo, pp.1-19.
'PROSPECTIVE REVIEW' (1853), Society in danger from children,

'Prospective Review', vol.9.
READER, D. (1979), Industry and education, in G. Bernbaum (ed.), 'Schooling in Decline', London: Macmillan.
RIDLEY, P.F. (1981), Youth on Merseyside, 'Political Quarterly', vol.52, no.1 pp.16-27.
ROBINS, D. and COHEN, P. (1978), 'Knuckle Sandwich', Harmondsworth: Penguin.
RUSSELL, C.E.B. (1905), 'Manchester Boys', Manchester University Press.
SEABROOK, J. (1973), 'City Close-Up', Harmondsworth: Penguin.
SEABROOK, J. (1981), Unemployment now and in the 1930s, 'Political Quarterly', 52 (1) pp.7-15.
SEYMOUR, J.B. (1928), 'The British Employment Exchange', London: Allen & Unwin.
SIMON, B. (1974), 'The Politics of Education Reform, 1920-1940', London: Lawrence & Wishart.
STEDMAN JONES, G. (1971), 'Outcast London: A Study in the Relationship Between Classes in Victorian Society', London: Oxford University Press.
TAWNEY, R.H. (1909), Economics of boy labour, 'Economic Journal', 19, pp.517-37.
TAWNEY, R.H. (1922), 'Secondary Education for All', London: Allen & Unwin.
TAWNEY, R.H. (1928), 'The Possible Cost of Raising the School Leaving Age', London: Labour Party.
TAWNEY, R.H. (1973), Keep the workers' children in their places, reprinted in W. Van Der Gyken (ed.), 'Education, The Child and Society', Harmondsworth: Penguin.
TAYLOR, P. (1979), Daughters and mothers - maids and mistresses: domestic service between the wars, in J. Clarke, C. Critcher and R. Johnson (eds), 'Working-class Culture', London: Hutchinson.
THOMPSON, E.P. (1968), 'The Making of the English Working Class', Harmondsworth: Penguin.
'TIMES EDUCATIONAL SUPPLEMENT' (1976), What the PM said, 'TES', 22 October.
TOBIAS, J.J. (1967), 'Crime and Industrial Society in the Nineteenth Century', Harmondsworth: Penguin.
TUC (1972), 'Annual Report', London: TUC.
TUC (1978), 'A Chance Would be a Fine Thing', London: TUC.
TUC (1981a), 'Unemployment: the Fight for TUC Alternatives', London: TUC.
TUC (1981b), 'Economic Review', London: TUC.
URWICK, E.J. (ed.) (1904), 'Studies of Boy Life in Our Cities', London: Dent.
WHITE, J. (1981), The summer riots of 1919, 'New Society', 57 (978), pp.260-1.
WILLIAMSON, H. (1979), 'Social policy, state intervention and youth unemployment' (mimeo), Social Evaluation Unit, University of Oxford.
WILLIAMSON, H. (1980), 'The aims and possibilities of the youth opportunities programme' (mimeo), Social Evaluation Unit, University of Oxford.
WILLIS, P. (1977), 'Learning to Labour: How Working Class Kids Get

Working Class Jobs', Farnborough: Saxon House.
YOUTH EMPLOYMENT RESOURCE UNIT (1980), 'Worknet', no.1, July
1980, Birmingham: YERU.

INDEX